Latin American Monographs

Second Series

Colombia's Foreign Trade
and Economic Integration
in Latin America

9

Center for Latin American Studies
University of Florida

Colombia's Foreign Trade and Economic Integration in Latin America

J. Kamal Dow

University of Florida Press
Gainesville - 1971

Latin American Monographs—Second Series

A University of Florida Press Publication

SPONSORED BY THE
CENTER FOR LATIN AMERICAN STUDIES

Series design by Stanley D. Harris

Library of Congress
Catalog Card No. 71-631067
ISBN 0-8130-0308-3

PRINTED BY STORTER PRINTING COMPANY
  GAINESVILLE, FLORIDA

Contents

v

Tables

Introduction

SHORTLY AFTER the Montevideo Treaty was signed in February, 1960, Colombia decided to join the Latin American Free Trade Association (LAFTA). Since then that country has become one of the most enthusiastic supporters of Latin American integration. The number of trade concessions granted so far and, more important, the evolution of its trade figures compared with those of the rest of the countries in the region show beyond any doubt that Colombia is one of the most "integrationist" countries in the area. Its willingness to expedite the process of economic integration was further demonstrated by the leadership Colombia displayed in the negotiations leading to the formation of the Andean Group.

At the time of Colombia's entrance into LAFTA it was thought that the country could only gain from such a partnership. The optimistic atmosphere prevailing in the economic spheres and in the decision-making hierarchy was much like that prevailing throughout the region. The trade figures of the last few years, however, show that in certain cases the reciprocity that was implicit in the Montevideo Treaty has not existed. They also show that most of the gains have been through trade with the countries of the Andean Group and that Colombia's dependence on trade partners from outside the region has not decreased as rapidly as was expected.

1

The developments that have taken place in the integration process will be discussed in chapter 1. From them, it will become evident that the LAFTA countries will be facing crucial issues in negotiations in the near future. Thus, this seems to be the right time for each country to stop and take a thorough analytical look at its present position relative to each of the other countries and to the region as a whole. It may prove useful in providing some guides as to what the future policy of integration should be. This study does that for Colombia.

Data and Procedure

There were three main sources of data consulted in this study. Statistics concerning gross domestic product, income, and balance of payments for Colombia were taken from the National Account Statistics published by the Banco de la República, which is considered the official source of financial data. Statistics on Colombian imports and exports by country and by commodity were taken from several issues of *Boletín Mensual de Estadísticas* and *Anuario de Comercio Exterior*, both published by the Departamento Administrativo Nacional de Estadística (DANE), the official Colombian statistical agency. Figures on intra-LAFTA trade were taken from several issues of *Síntesis Mensual,* an official publication of the secretariat of LAFTA.

Since Venezuela and Bolivia did not join LAFTA until 1967, official LAFTA publications do not include statistics on these two countries. They are therefore excluded from the intra-LAFTA trade figures. Colombia's trade with Venezuela was included in the analysis and the data were taken from DANE's publications. Colombia's trade with Bolivia has been negligible (less than $8,000[1] per year) and will not be considered here.

In order to analyze Colombia's position in LAFTA, the study starts in chapter 1 by describing the conditions prevailing in Latin America during the late fifties which led to the signing of the Montevideo Treaty. A short summary of the basic provisions of the treaty is provided and the main developments and difficulties that LAFTA has encountered are described, followed by a discussion of the model to be used in this study. A general description of Colombia follows in chapter 2, which points out some of the main physical and social characteristics which have affected the country's economic development as described in chapter 3. There the evolution

1. All dollar signs indicate American dollars.

of some of the main economic indicators is observed and the structure and development of the important agricultural sector are analyzed. Chapter 4 analyzes the development, structure, and characteristics of the manufacturing sector, which is of vital importance in the integration process. The competitiveness of this sector is also studied.

Chapter 5 is an analysis of the foreign trade of Colombia, its evolution through the years, its product composition, and its geographic structure. A product by product analysis of the destination of the most important exports is made. Intraregional trade is analyzed in chapter 6 and the importance of each country to that trade is studied as well as each country's trade balance with Colombia. The evolution of the trade of Colombia with the region is analyzed on a country by country basis in an effort to observe the effect that liberalization has had on regional trade. Chapter 7 summarizes the findings of the previous chapters and suggests the route that should be taken regarding economic integration.

Limitations

The conclusions of this study have been based on the analysis of the trade that has taken place since the Montevideo Treaty started to take effect. This is indeed a short time and therefore any conclusions as to future behavior based on past trends carries the possibility of considerable error. This same fact precludes the use of sophisticated techniques to make extrapolations of the data either with single equations or by building a trade matrix for the LAFTA countries. Furthermore, the present state of development of Latin American industry would make it very difficult to forecast what the future composition of intra-LAFTA trade would be.

Augmenting the two limitations mentioned above is the fact that economic considerations are being applied to some developments which have been basically a result of political decisions. Many of those decisions may be prompted by social pressures and the subsequent commitments of the governments to protect existing structures, either industrial or institutional, regardless of the costs that in the long run may have to be paid in terms of inefficient resource allocation or even lower welfare. It is the role of the economist to try to take into consideration the possible impact of those decisions and even to try to predict their occurrence. Based on the belief that political decisions will be favorable, it is recommended that the route of faster integration with the Andean Group be followed.

1. Trade, Integration, and the Economic Model

T HE THEORY of international trade is merely an application of general economic theory to the study of trade between countries. It could also be applied to the study of trade between groups of countries or between regions of the same country, but the emphasis has usually been placed on trade between separate nations. Several factors account for this emphasis; some of them are economic in nature while others are social or political. Among the economic factors are: the differences that exist in mobility of the factors of production within a country as compared with mobility of those factors between countries; the restrictions to trade in the form of tariffs or quotas are usually different in every nation, whereas they do not exist within a nation; the restrictions placed on international capital transactions; and the fact that the economic infrastructure as represented by transportation facilities, energy sources, and the like is generally more homogeneous within a country. The social and political characteristics are also more homogeneous within a country since all individuals and firms share the same economic institutions, the same legal framework, and usually the same background.

The formal study of international trade originated with the economists of the classical school. Although not contributing directly to the theory of international trade, Adam Smith was one of the first to inquire extensively into the principles governing the division of labor.[1] Smith's work contributed to the disappearance of the mercantilist feelings of his contemporaries and helped to clear the way for the acceptance of classical theory and the free trade policy. His influence was an extension of that of David Hume, who, twenty-four years earlier, had written his famous essay *On the Balance of Trade*.[2]

Three-quarters of a century later, John Stuart Mill spoke again of the advantages of trade among nations. He criticized Adam Smith's implication that exports were mainly an outlet for surplus and maintained that "the only direct advantage of foreign commerce consists in the imports." According to Mill, by importing, "a country obtains things which it either could not have produced at all, or which it must have produced at a greater expense of capital and labor than the costs of the things which it exports to pay for them."[3]

Both Adam Smith and John Stuart Mill based their arguments on principles of absolute advantage. David Ricardo was the first to base his analysis of the advantages of trade on the principle of comparative advantage which he called "comparative cost."

His model was based on one input, labor, two commodities, and two countries. His main assumptions were free mobility of goods between countries, free mobility of factors of production within a country, but no mobility of factors between countries.[4]

Comparative cost analysis sets the limits within which the terms of trade will be set. Determination of the exact terms of trade requires a knowledge of the interaction of supply and demand, which became known as the theory of "international values" developed by Marshall, who used geometric and analytical techniques.[5]

The classical economists broke the ground for the study of the problems of international trade. Since their time, many economists have inquired into the different aspects related to trade between

1. Adam Smith, *An Inquiry into the Nature and Causes of the Wealth of Nations*.
2. Reprinted in *International Trade Theory*, ed. William Allen.
3. John Stuart Mill, *Principles of Political Economy*.
4. David Ricardo, *The Principles of Political Economy and Taxation*, chapter 7.
5. Alfred Marshall, *The Pure Theory of Foreign Trade*.

nations such as the balance of payments, trade policy, the welfare effects of trade, and the theory of economic integration. Of special interest for this study is the problem of economic integration and the role that it plays in the economic growth of a country.

Latin American Integration and Economic Development

The importance of diversification of production and an even income distribution notwithstanding, economic development can be briefly defined as an increase in total and per capita output of an economy. In order for economic development to occur, there must be an increase in the stock of capital and an improvement in the technological process. In the works of Harrod[6] and Domar,[7] the emphasis was placed on the rate of capital formation. Some empirical studies have shown that technological improvements explain a considerable portion of the increase in output.[8] The two variables should be considered as being interrelated since in general the application of new technology presupposes an increase in the stock of capital, while at the same time the adoption of new methods of production permits faster capital accumulation.

The concern over economic development in Latin America reached considerable proportions during the late fifties. After the end of World War II, and until the mid-fifties, the rate of growth had been satisfactory. From 1945 to 1955 the gross national product (GNP) of the region increased by 65 per cent, and the per capita GNP increased by 31 per cent. On a cumulative basis, then, per capita GNP grew at an annual rate of 2.75 per cent, higher than the present goals of the Alliance for Progress. During that same period, the per capita consumption increased by 40 per cent and imports of goods and services by 130 per cent (Table 1).

The economic growth of Latin America during the decade of 1945–55 can be explained at least in part by the fact that the region was able to satisfy the increasing requirements of capital necessary to finance its development. Gross domestic fixed capital formation increased from an annual average of $5.3 billion during the period 1945–47 to an average of $8.1 billion during 1953–55. Nearly 30 per cent of total investment during the period consisted of machinery and equipment.

6. Roy Harrod, "An Essay in Dynamic Theory."
7. Evsey D. Domar, "Expansion and Employment."
8. See for example R. M. Solow, "Technical Change and the Aggregate Production Function."

Since Latin America depends a great deal on imports from outside the area to satisfy its requirements for machinery and equipment, it follows that in order to finance the development, its transactions with the rest of the world must show a favorable balance. This was true during the 1945–55 period and three factors contributed to it.

First, and most important, was the improvement of the terms of trade caused by the increase in demand for most products after the war ended. It is estimated that the purchasing power of the Latin

TABLE 1

LATIN AMERICA: GROSS NATIONAL PRODUCT, POPULATION, CONSUMPTION, INVESTMENT, EXPORTS, AND IMPORTS, 1945–55 (ALL DOLLAR FIGURES AT 1950 PRICES)

Year	Gross National Product (Billion U.S. $)	Population (Million)	Per Capita GNP (U.S. $)	Investment (Billion U.S. $)	Exports	Imports
					(Billion U.S. $)	
1945	30.2	138.5	218	4.0	6.7	3.6
1946	32.8	141.6	232	5.0	7.4	4.8
1947	34.4	144.9	237	6.8	7.2	7.1
1948	36.4	148.2	246	6.8	7.5	6.6
1949	37.6	151.8	248	6.4	6.9	5.9
1950	39.8	155.4	256	6.6	7.2	6.1
1951	42.1	159.2	264	7.4	7.1	7.5
1952	43.0	163.1	264	7.6	6.9	6.9
1953	44.7	166.9	268	7.6	7.8	6.9
1954	47.3	170.9	277	8.2	7.7	7.8
1955	50.0	175.1	286	8.6	8.4	8.1

SOURCES: United Nations, Economic Commission for Latin America, and *Boletín Estadístico de America Latina*, several issues.

American exports increased at an annual rate of more than 5 per cent during the decade under consideration. The second factor was import substitution, which became important due to the impossibility of obtaining certain products during the war. Third, a considerable inflow of foreign capital helped the balance of payments of most Latin American countries.

By the second half of the fifties, the situation started to change. The prices of the primary products of Latin America started to decline and its terms of trade to deteriorate. This condition has continued into the present and there is no sign that this trend will be reversed any time in the future. A close examination of the present world situation and future perspectives shows that the demand for the traditional Latin American exports is not apt to increase at a rate that would support the same level of economic growth. Even if the most optimistic projections are realized and the demand for Latin America's basic products increases at a rate of 4 per cent per year, it is very doubtful that the relative prices of those exports will ever reach the levels of the postwar decade. This dimension of the trade process as the primary source for providing the necessary capital must be abandoned if the situation is to be observed realistically.

With prices for its products declining in the world market, the most immediate alternative to follow to maintain a desirable rate of growth was that of increased import substitution. Most Latin American countries seemed to become aware of this fact and encouraged the local manufacture of many products which up to then were imported. The new enterprises were protected and encouraged by high import tariffs and quotas.

As time passed, however, the governments also became aware that import substitution was encountering more and more difficulties. The larger countries, enjoying rather ample markets, had by the late fifties substituted almost all imports of consumer goods that were possible within reasonable economic limits. On the other hand, the countries with smaller markets were consuming 60 per cent of all such goods imported into Latin America, and, with very few exceptions, any further substitution would have been very expensive. The same problem of high costs was to be found by the larger countries in the cases of industries requiring large capital investments and characterized by economies of large-scale production.

Thus, the Latin American countries decided that the best alternative would be the substitution of imports within the framework of a common market or trade association. This course of action combined with international financing would allow Latin America to reduce its demand for goods from outside the area to a level consistent with the availability of foreign exchange and at the same time improve its technology, thus taking advantage of specialization and the economies of large-scale production.

It was this consideration and, to some extent, the success of the European Economic Community and the European Free Trade Association that prompted the Latin American countries to move toward some kind of economic integration. The first experiment of this kind, which it seems to have developed into a rather successful integration movement, was the Central American Common

Market (CACM). The second effort along these lines is the Latin American Free Trade Association (LAFTA). Born in Montevideo in February, 1960, LAFTA encompasses all the South American countries and Mexico.

The ideology of economic development in Latin America can be found in the writings of many Latin American economists such as Urquidi, Furtado, and Wionczeck, to mention just a few. Their works are listed in the bibliography. Similarly, integration has been the subject of several studies and essays by Balassa (*El Desarrollo Económico y la Integración*), De Aguiar (*Fundamentos, Objectivos e Bases do Mercado Regional Latino-Americano*), Dell (*Problemas de un Mercado Común en Latina América*), Wionczeck (*Integración de la América Latina*), and many others, but the most important is Raul Prebish, whose line of thought became known as the Economic Commission for Latin America's line of thought. It was Prebish, who, as secretary of the commission, first became concerned about the fact that the less developed countries (the "periphery" as he called them) were growing at a much slower rate than the wealthy ones; his influence was decisive in the shaping of LAFTA. The essence of Prebish's arguments can be found in the United Nations publication entitled *Bases para la Formación de un Mercado Común Latino-Americano*.

The Treaty of Montevideo

According to the terms of the Treaty of Montevideo, the contracting countries committed themselves to the gradual elimination of tariffs and restrictions affecting the importation of products originating "in the territory of any Contracting Party."[9] The elimination of tariffs and restrictions was scheduled to be accomplished over a period of twelve years and was to encompass all kinds of restrictions, including those on foreign exchange or any type of fiscal or monetary measures.

The above objectives were to be implemented by means of two schedules. The first, entitled the National Schedule, was to include the products on which each party would grant concessions to the other members after an annual negotiating meeting. The yearly reduction of tariffs for products in this schedule was planned to be at least 8 per cent of the weighted average of the current tariffs as applicable to third countries. The second, entitled the Common

9. Asociación Latino Americana de Libre Comercio, *Tratado de Montevideo, Resoluciones de la Conferencia,* article 3.

Schedule, was to include a list of products whose tariffs would be eliminated over a period of twelve years. According to the treaty, by the end of the first three years this schedule must include products which account for at least 25 per cent of the total value of trade. And, after six, nine, and twelve years, the Common Schedule must include, respectively, 50 per cent, 75 per cent, and "essentially all"[10] of the trade between the member countries.

The inclusion of a product in the Common Schedule was irreversible. However, the products included in the National Schedule could be withdrawn after agreement between the affected parties and provided that "adequate compensation"[11] was given.

One of the provisions of the treaty authorized member countries to permit one another to temporarily restrict imports of a particular negotiated item whenever those imports threatened an industry which was deemed to be of strategic importance to the national economy. Restrictions imposed on this basis must be nondiscriminatory. Also, the treaty contained provisions for imposing restrictions in order to avoid significant balance of payments difficulties.

Because of the vital role that agriculture plays in all the countries, special provisions to deal with this sector of the economy were provided in the treaty. An intention was that member countries would coordinate their agricultural development policies in their best interest without disrupting each other's productive patterns. The restrictive measures applied to agricultural products are supposed to only limit imports to the difference between consumption and local production or to bring the level of prices of imported commodities to the level of prices of locally produced ones.

Because of the difference in size and economic development among the member countries, provisions were made to grant certain preferences to the less developed countries. These countries would be permitted to reduce their tariffs over longer periods of time, and the larger countries were encouraged to provide the small ones with technical and financial assistance.[12] Initially, Ecuador, Bolivia, and Paraguay were classed as less developed countries, and, in 1967, Uruguay was added to this group.

In 1963, a new category of countries within LAFTA was created. It was called "countries of insufficient market" and included Colombia, Chile, Peru, and Uruguay; Venezuela was added in 1966.

10. Ibid., article 7.
11. Ibid., article 8.
12. Ibid., article 32.

These countries, although more developed than Paraguay, Bolivia, and Ecuador, do not enjoy markets as ample as the larger countries of the region; consequently their industrial sector, it was argued, could not effectively compete with the giants. The advantages that the countries in this classification will enjoy have not been specified yet, but they are expected to be extended to the smallest countries of the group.

From Success in Montevideo to Failure in Asunción

The process of integration proved to be easy only at the beginning. It was easy, for example, for Argentina to eliminate its barriers to the entry of Colombian or Brazilian coffee or Chilean and Peruvian copper, both products not produced locally. It did not imply a sacrifice for Brazil to allow free entry of Argentina's wheat or for Chile to allow the free entry of Argentina's beef or Peruvian sugar. The inclusion of products that accounted for 25 per cent of the value of intraregional trade was successfully completed on schedule.

When the list of products that were traditionally traded ran out, however, the difficulties started. After 1964, it became apparent that fulfilling the second set of requirements of the Common List would not be an easy task, and the many obstacles to integration, which had previously remained in the background, started to become obvious. Suddenly, most members began to appear more concerned about the differences in economic development between the countries as well as the uneven rates of growth of the different economies. The difficulties resulting from the inadequate transportation facilities prevailing through the region were mentioned more often, the inadequacy of the existing mechanisms for the clearing of payments began to be stressed, and concern about the existence of overvalued and undervalued currencies grew rapidly.

The situation culminated with the Asunción meeting in mid-1967 in which the foreign ministers of the LAFTA countries failed to agree on most of the issues discussed. This meeting was concerned with the liberalization of trade, with a Latin American Common Market encompassing both LAFTA and CACM in sight. This failure was an ominous prelude to the Ordinary Meeting held in Montevideo in December, 1967, at which LAFTA failed completely to fulfill its old commitment of completing the second stage of the Common List negotiations.

As a reaction to the slow development of LAFTA, a movement

was started by the more integrationist countries. In 1966, in Bogota, the presidents of Colombia, Ecuador, Peru, Chile, and Venezuela announced their determination to create an Andean common market within LAFTA. Besides a faster removal of tariffs among the participating countries, this movement would include complementarity agreements in many important industries and attempts to coordinate development, exchange, financial, foreign trade, and investment policies. Special provisions were contemplated for Ecuador and Bolivia, which joined the bloc at a later stage.

The Economic Model

The previous discussion has provided the foundations for the inquiry which will be the central topic of this study. It was stated above that concern over economic growth was the main force behind Latin American integration. It was also stated that to achieve economic growth there must be an increase in the stock of capital and an improvement in the level of technology. It follows, then, that in order for a country (Colombia in this case) to benefit from it, integration must contribute to the attainment of these two objectives.

Technological change has been mentioned, but has not been defined. If it is defined as an upward shift in the aggregate production function, then it is equivalent to what Balassa calls dynamic efficiency: "The movement of the production-possibility frontier in the north-east direction."[13] The same author classifies the factors that affect it under two headings: large-scale economies and autonomous technological change.[14]

The first assumption of the model concerns technological change. It will be assumed that the increase in the size of the market resulting from economic integration will result in large-scale economies, but no attempt will be made to measure this impact. Furthermore, autonomous technological change will be assumed to be imported, or in other words, external to and independent of the events that take place in the region. This seems to be a reasonable assumption, since large allocations of resources to research expenditures are the exception rather than the rule, at least at the present time.

Colombian production of capital goods is negligible; therefore, the country depends on imports in order to supply its needs of pro-

13. Bela Balassa, *The Theory of Economic Integration*, p. 13.
14. Ibid., p. 103.

ductive equipment. It follows then, that any increase in the capital stock will depend on the country's capacity to import, which is reflected by the foreign exchange availability. A country can obtain foreign exchange either by exporting goods and services, or by long-term borrowing (short-term borrowing and gold sales are considered compensatory movements). Long-term borrowing, however, is limited by the country's capacity to repay, and its extended use may drive the country to a situation in which the servicing of the foreign debt is of such magnitude that it will absorb most of what can be obtained by way of new loans. Export of goods and services is the most desirable, the least burdensome, and, in many cases, the only readily available way of obtaining foreign exchange.

Because of Colombia's stage of economic development, export of services is negligible in comparison with export of goods; thus, this study concentrates on the latter. Exports of goods can be broken down into two general categories: raw materials and manufactured goods. This classification is useful because raw materials in the case of Colombia are composed mainly of food items, the increase in the demand for which is proportional to the increase in population, and consequently slow, plus the fact that most countries in the area produce competitive food products. Exports of manufactures, in contrast, are of a more dynamic character. Therefore, it is very important to look not only at the change in value of exports, but at their structure. Exports are only part of the story, however, and to get a complete picture of the impact of integration on the foreign trade of Colombia, it is necessary to look at both imports and exports, or, in other words, at the trade balance.

To summarize what has been said in this section then, the foreign trade sector is the main determinant of foreign exchange availability. The availability of foreign exchange determines the country's ability to obtain productive equipment and, consequently, increase its stock of capital. The increase in capital formation in turn determines, *ceteris paribus,* the rate of growth of the country. This study will look at the foreign trade sector of Colombia and analyze the role that economic integration has played in that sector.

2. General Description of Colombia

COLOMBIA is located in the northwest corner of South America. It has an area of 445,000 square miles and is the only country in South America with coasts on both the Pacific and the Atlantic oceans. The length of its border is 5,740 miles, of which 800 miles correspond to the Pacific shoreline, 1,000 miles to the Atlantic shoreline, and the rest to international borders with Venezuela and Brazil to the east, Peru and Ecuador to the south, and Panama to the northwest.

Climate

Because of its latitude, Colombia possesses a tropical climate, and the differences in mean temperature among regions are determined by the topography and mainly by the altitude above sea level. There are no seasonal variations in temperature, but some variation (although never over 30° F) exists in the daily temperature.

There is a wide variation in the distribution of rainfall. Some regions in the department of Guajira have an annual average precipitation of 13 inches, while some parts of Choco receive 400 inches of rain every year. Because of its location between the two oceans, and because it is crossed by large rivers, the humidity is generally high. Some selvatic regions and some areas on the Pacific coast have humidities that vary from 75 to 90 per cent all year round.

Population and Population Growth

According to the last census, taken in 1964, the population of Colombia was 17,484,508 as compared with 11,484,172 in 1951. The annual cumulative rate of growth of population between the two census years was 3.25 per cent, which is higher than the Latin American average of 2.9 per cent estimated by the Economic Commission for Latin America.[1] There are some indications, however, that the rate of growth is decreasing and presently may be in the neighborhood of 3.0 per cent. If this tendency continues, the population should reach the 20 million mark sometime in 1969. This high rate of growth is common to most developing nations, and the reason for it is well known. The birth rate has increased slightly from 36.3 per thousand in 1951 to 38.6 per thousand in 1964, while advances in medical technology and health services and care have reduced the mortality rate from 14.3 per thousand in 1951 to about 10.0 per thousand in 1964. Most striking is the reduction in infant mortality which dropped from 120 per thousand to 83 per thousand during the thirteen years between the two census dates.

Urban and Rural Population

If the distribution of population between urban and rural is analyzed, a clearly marked tendency toward urbanization can be observed. Table 2 shows that urban population, which represented less than 30 per cent in 1938, accounted for over one-half of the total population by 1964. From the figures in the table it can be seen that the increase in population was unevenly distributed among the urban and the rural sectors. Furthermore, this tendency seems to be getting stronger. During the period 1938–51 the annual cumulative rate of growth was 4.3 per cent for urban population and 1.2 per cent for rural population. This difference widened during the 1951–64 period when the rate for urban growth increased to 5.8 per cent while that for rural growth remained at 1.2 per cent.

The tide of political violence that swept the Colombian countryside during the fifties greatly influenced the migration of rural families to the outskirts of urban areas. Other forces behind this tre-

1. United Nations, Economic Commission for Latin America, *Economic Survey of Latin America,* p. 47.

mendous urbanization process were the new opportunities for employment that opened due to the industrialization process and the desire of the rural workers for higher money incomes and better opportunities for their children.

This process of urban concentration has taken place in a way that may be considered *sui generis* in Latin America. Although in most Latin American countries rural–urban migration is concentrated around one or two cities, the urbanization phenomenon in Colombia has been spread over more than a dozen urban centers.

As Table 3 shows, there is one city with a little less than 10 per cent of the total population and two with less than 5 per cent each; the rest of the major cities have populations ranging between 0.6

TABLE 2

URBAN AND RURAL POPULATION

Census Year	Population				
	Total	Urban	%	Rural	%
1938	8,701,816	2,533,680	29.1	6,168,136	70.9
1951	11,548,172	4,468,437	38.7	7,079,735	61.3
1964	17,484,508	9,093,094	52.0	8,391,414	48.0

SOURCES: DANE, *Censo de Población de Colombia 1951, Resumen*, pp. 13, 16; and *Censo Nacional de Población, Julio 15 de 1964, Resumen General*, p. 29.

TABLE 3

COLOMBIAN CITIES OF MORE THAN 100,000 INHABITANTS

City	Population
Bogotá	1,697,311
Medellín	772,887
Cali	637,929
Barranquilla	498,301
Cartagena	242,085
Bucaramanga	229,748
Manizales	221,916
Pereira	188,365
Cúcuta	175,336
Ibagué	163,661
Palmira	140,889
Armenia	137,222
Montería	126,329
Cienaga	113,143
Pasto	112,876
Santa Marta	104,471

SOURCE: DANE, *Censo Nacional de Población, Julio 15 de 1964, Resumen General*, pp. 30, 32.

per cent and 2.8 per cent of the total. A migration of this type is less apt to cause severe hardships due to scarcity of services, slum dwellings, and the like. This situation contrasts sharply with that prevailing throughout the rest of Latin America, where, with the exception of Brazil, there are only two or three important urban centers in each country. Expansion of the national market and economic and social pressures for better transportation networks are liable to be stronger in Colombia than in any other country in Latin America.

Economically Active Population

Due to the factors mentioned earlier about birth and mortality rates, and improved health conditions, there has been an increase in the percentage of the population between the ages of one and fourteen years, which has caused the percentage of potentially active population to decline from 33 to 29 per cent of the total, between the census years of 1951 and 1964.

The distributions of the economically active population by sectors of economic activity for the census years of 1951 and 1961 are shown in Table 4. It is a significant fact that the percentage of the active population in agriculture and other primary activities de-

TABLE 4

DISTRIBUTION OF ECONOMICALLY ACTIVE POPULATION BY SECTORS OF ECONOMIC
ACTIVITY (CENSUSES OF 1951 AND 1964)

Activity	1951 Census		1964 Census		Increase
	Persons	%	Persons	%	%
Total	3,755,609	100.0	5,134,125	100.0	+36.7
Agriculture, forestry, hunting, and fishing	2,023,281	53.9	2,427,059	47.3	+20.0
Mines and quarries	61,223	1.6	50,279	1.0	−17.9
Construction	132,922	3.5	220,705	4.3	+66.0
Manufacturing	460,907	12.3	686,961	13.4	+49.0
Utilities, (electricity, water, gas, sewerage, etc.)	10,472	0.3	13,276	0.3	+26.8
Commerce	203,774	5.4	440,520	8.6	+116.2
Transportation and communications	130,083	3.5	191,817	3.7	+47.5
Services	598,093	15.9	925,946	18.0	+54.8
Nonspecified	134,854	3.6	177,562	3.4	+31.7

SOURCE: DANE, Censo de Población de Colombia 1951, Resumen, p. 138; and DANE, Censo Nacional de Población, Julio 15 de 1964, Resumen General, pp. 124–29.

creased from 55.5 to 48.3, or 7.2 percentage points, while the percentage employed in manufacturing and construction increased by only 1.9 percentage points. This seems to indicate that those two sectors have a low absorption capacity of the labor released by the agricultural sector. Commerce and services absorbed a relatively large proportion of labor.

Health

In spite of the fact that significant progress has been made in the field of health, much remains to be done. Among the results of the advances made, it must be mentioned that life expectancy has increased from forty-five to fifty-three years over the last decade. The decreases in the mortality rate, both adult and infant, also play an important role. On the other hand, sanitary facilities are scarce or nonexistent in a great percentage of the rural areas. The daily caloric intake averages about 2,100 or 80 per cent of the required subsistence level. Besides this quantitative deficit, there is a qualitative one since most of the diet is based on products with high starch content, and the consumption of meat, eggs, milk, and animal proteins is generally very low.

Literacy

The literacy rate in Colombia increased from 57 to 73 per cent of the total population between 1951 and 1964. Although this is a considerable improvement and puts the country in a better position than many other Latin American nations, it still compares unfavorably with countries like Argentina, Uruguay, and Chile. Most of the illiteracy occurs in the rural areas where, for obvious reasons, education is less accessible than in the cities. Table 5 shows the 1964 census figures for urban and rural literacy rates.

TABLE 5
LITERACY RATES (1964 CENSUS)

	Population Age 15 and Over (Thousands)	Urban		Rural	
		Persons	%	Persons	%
Total	9,329	5,029	100.0	4,300	100.0
Literates	6,802	4,277	85.0	2,525	58.4
Illiterates	2,527	752	15.0	1,775	41.6

SOURCE: DANE, *Censo Nacional de Población, Julio 15 de 1964, Resumen General*, p. 74.

The increasing preoccupation of the Colombian government with the problem of illiteracy is encouraging and can be shown by the fact that although in 1951 only 40 per cent of the school-age children were enrolled in schools this percentage increased to 60 per cent by 1966.[2] It is estimated that if the present rate of increase in school enrollment continues, by 1985, 90 per cent of the school-age children will be attending school.

2. DANE, *Anuario General de Estadística* (1967).

3. The Economy and Its Development

TABLE 6 shows the behavior of gross domestic product (GDP) from 1950 to 1967, both at current market prices and at constant 1958 prices. It can be observed that in real terms the period of fastest growth was from 1950 to 1955. During this time, GDP increased at an average rate of 5.3 per cent per year on a total basis and at an average rate of 2.2 per cent per year on a per capita basis. On the other hand, the five-year period from 1956 to 1960 showed a lower rate of growth in GDP of 4.0 per cent per year and a slightly higher rate of population growth which resulted in an average yearly increment of less than 1.0 per cent per year in per capita GDP. From 1961 to 1967 the economy showed a slight recovery, growing at an average rate of 4.3 per cent per year while the growth in population was slightly over 3.0 per cent, resulting in an average increase of 1.3 per cent per year in GDP per capita.

The value of the GDP of Colombia is greatly influenced by the price that agricultural exports, mainly coffee, command in world markets. The period 1950–55 was one of unusually high prices for those products and in this sense can be considered atypical. Because of this, a trend line based on the figures from 1956 and later is more representative of the long-run tendency. If the period from 1956 to 1967 is analyzed we can observe rates of growth of

4.2 per cent and 1.0 per cent per year for total GDP and per capita
GDP, respectively.

Structure of Gross Domestic Product

There has been some variation in the composition of the GDP
over the period 1950–67 both when each sector is considered sepa-
rately and when the sectors of economic activity are grouped according to whether they produce primary goods, secondary goods,
or utilities and services. Table 7 shows the percentages that each

TABLE 6

TOTAL AND PER CAPITA GROSS DOMESTIC PRODUCT, 1950–67

Year	Current Prices Total (Million Pesos)	1958 Prices Total (Million Pesos)	Per Capita (Pesos)
1950	7,861	14,689	1,310
1951	8,941	15,147	1,320
1952	9,651	16,102	1,360
1953	10,735	17,081	1,400
1954	12,759	18,262	1,450
1955	13,250	18,976	1,460
1956	14,863	19,746	1,470
1957	17,811	20,186	1,440
1958	20,682	20,682	1,430
1959	23,472	22,129	1,470
1960	26,418	23,042	1,490
1961	30,067	24,179	1,510
1962	33,578	25,396	1,550
1963	42,707	26,238	1,560
1964	52,700	27,812	1,590
1965	58,837	28,702	1,600
1966	61,956	30,056	1,620
1967[a]	65,000	31,000	1,630

SOURCES: Banco de la República, *Cuentas Nacionales*, several issues. United
Nations Economic Commission for Latin America, *Statistical Bulletin of Latin
America*, vol. 3, no. 1.
    a. Estimate.

sector contributed to the total for the average of four five-year
periods in 1950, 1955, 1960, and 1965.

From the aggregate sectors it can be observed that the primary
goods-producing sector has reduced its participation in the economy from 38.4 to 32.8 per cent over a period of fifteen years and
that the reduction has taken place at a rather uniform rate. On the
other hand, the secondary goods-producing sector increased its
participation very slightly, going from 20.4 to 22.8 per cent of the
total over the period with most of the increase taking place at a

uniform rate throughout the last decade. The goods-producing sectors taken together had decreased participation in the economy, going from 58.8 to 55.6 per cent of the total. The sectors that produce utilities and services increased their participation in the economy with most of the increase taking place during the last five years considered.

The changes in the structure of the aggregate sectors that form the GDP can be observed by looking at the different sectors that form those aggregates. The agriculture and livestock subsector

TABLE 7

COMPOSITION OF GROSS DOMESTIC PRODUCT BY SECTOR OF ECONOMIC ACTIVITY

Sector	5-Year Average Centered at			
	1950	1955	1960	1965
Total	100.0	100.0	100.0	100.0
Good-Producing	58.8	57.2	58.1	55.6
Primary	38.4	36.6	36.4	32.8
Agriculture and livestock	35.9	34.1	32.1	29.6
Fishing and hunting	0.2	0.1	0.2	0.3
Mining	2.0	2.1	3.7	2.5
Forestry	0.3	0.3	0.4	0.4
Secondary	20.4	20.6	21.7	22.8
Manufacturing	17.8	17.0	18.2	19.3
Construction	2.6	3.6	3.5	3.5
Utilities and Services	41.2	42.8	41.9	44.4
Commerce	13.5	14.5	14.9	14.4
Transport	6.5	6.6	5.3	5.2
Communications	0.4	0.5	0.6	0.8
Electricity, gas, and water	0.5	0.7	0.9	1.3
Banks, insurance, and financing	1.7	2.1	2.5	3.2
Net housing rent	6.6	5.7	5.4	6.1
Government services	4.3	5.2	5.2	5.8
Personal services	7.7	7.5	7.1	7.6

SOURCE: Banco de la República, *Cuentas Nacionales,* several issues.

which forms the bulk of the primary producing sector reduced its participation in the total from 35.9 to 29.6 per cent over the period considered, and this reduction has taken place uniformly throughout the period. The other primary producing sectors do not show any significant change although a slight increase in activity in all of them can be observed throughout the period. It is worthwhile noting that the mining sector showed a great increase from 1955 to 1960 and a substantial reduction from 1960 to 1965. Petroleum activity is included in this sector, and since there is no sign of its reduction, it must be concluded that the substantial reduction in activity has taken place through the rest of the mining sector.

Manufacturing constitutes the bulk of the secondary activities and after a slight decline from 1950 to 1955 it increased, but at a very slow rate. Total participation went from 17.8 per cent in 1950 to 19.3 per cent in 1965, a performance which leaves much to be desired and reflects on the one hand some difficulties of a domestic nature such as the reduced size of the market and the lack of available capital. On the other hand are some external factors, the most important of which is the chronic balance of payments difficulties which limit the country's capacity to import, and, consequently, hinder the efforts of the sector to obtain inputs and productive equipment. The construction sector performed very well from 1950 to 1955 when its participation in the total went from 2.6 to 3.6 per cent. Since then it has been stagnant, reflecting government policies aimed at freezing rents and reducing expenditures.

There were differences in the behavior of the different sectors that generate services. Steady increases are observed in the electricity, gas, and water sectors, reflecting the increased interest of the government in providing a better standard of living for the people, and in the banks, insurance, and financing sectors, reflecting a more sophisticated type of business activity. The traditional commerce sector has remained stagnant while participation of the transport sector in the economy has decreased.

Prices

The rate of increase of the level of prices to the consumer reflects the degree of the inflationary tendency in a country. Table 8 shows the behavior of prices in Colombia and compares it with the behavior in the other LAFTA countries. In the series for Colombia two periods are clearly distinguishable: a period of moderate increase in prices from 1950 to 1962 during which prices increased at a cumulative annual rate of 6.5 per cent, followed by a period of rapid inflation from 1962 to 1966 as consumer prices increased at an annual cumulative rate of 16.7 per cent. During 1967 the increase was only about 7 per cent, and this tendency seems to have continued through 1968. Preliminary figures show an increase of 6 per cent in the cost of living for this last year. The government is determined to hold the inflation rate down so that high rates like those of 1962–66 are not likely to occur during the next few years.

Comparison of the inflation rates in Colombia with those of the other LAFTA countries shows that in relative terms Colombia has experienced a moderate degree of inflation while some countries

TABLE 8

CONSUMER PRICES IN LAFTA COUNTRIES (INDEX 1958=100)

Country	1950	1955	1960	1961	1962	1963	1964	1965	1966	1967
Colombia	58	71	111	121	124	164	192	205	230	244
Argentina	23	54	272	309	396	491	600	771	909	1,120
Bolivia	1	16	134	144	153	152	167	175	187	195
Brazil	26	60	185	256	390	675	1,266	1,987	2,742	3,570
Chile	7	40	155	167	190	274	400	547	674	788
Ecuador	90	103	102	106	109	115	120	124	131	138
Mexico	53	81	108	109	111	111	114	116	117	119
Paraguay	8	67	119	141	143	146	149	155	159	161
Peru	58	82	122	107	114	121	134	154	164	180
Uruguay	41	69	194	237	263	316	452	708	1,229	2,326
Venezuela	91	97	109	106	105	106	107	109	109	108

SOURCES: United Nations, Economic Commission for Latin America, *Statistical Bulletin of Latin America*, vol. 3, no. 1; International Monetary Fund, *International Financial Statistics*.

such as Brazil and Argentina have shown cumulative annual rates of increase in prices of 49 per cent and 31 per cent, respectively, over the last decade. Others have shown very low rates, ranging from less than 1 per cent in Venezuela to 3.7 per cent in Ecuador. Over the same period, the rate for Colombia has been slightly over 10 per cent (see Table 9). The disparity of inflation rates throughout the region is remarkable.

The Balance of Payments

One of the biggest problems hampering Colombia's economic development and trade is the continuous deficit in its balance of payments. This deficit arises from an overdependence on unstable and

TABLE 9

ANNUAL CUMULATIVE RATES OF INCREASE IN CONSUMER PRICES FOR THE LAFTA COUNTRIES

Country	1950–62	1962–67	1958–67
Colombia	6.5	14.5	10.4
Argentina	26.5	23.1	31.0
Bolivia	53.0	5.0	6.9
Brazil	19.8	56.0	49.0
Chile	31.5	32.8	22.8
Ecuador	1.6	4.9	3.3
Mexico	6.3	1.4	1.8
Paraguay	27.2	2.4	5.4
Peru	5.8	9.6	6.1
Uruguay	16.8	54.0	41.9
Venezuela	1.2	1.0	1.0

SOURCE: Elaborated from figures in Table 8.

practically stagnant coffee exports and the consequent inability to augment imports sufficiently over a period of several years. Table 10 shows the behavior of the balance of payments since 1961. Only in two years (1965 and 1967) have there been increases in monetary reserves, and this was accomplished by large decreases (26.4 and 19.9 per cent, respectively) in imports, which, judging from the figures, came about as reactions to corresponding declines in the exports proceeds. This type of behavior is common. Being unable to affect international demand or prices for its exports, the country's only solutions are import restrictions, whatever form they may take.

A detailed discussion of the structure of the Colombian balance of payments will not be attempted here. It is necessary, however, to point out, as was just done, that this disequilibrium represents an important problem to which the government must react in some way. This topic will be discussed again in order to assess its importance and possible influence on the process of economic integration.

Sectors Most Affected by Economic Integration

The economic integration of Latin America will affect all the different sectors in the economy of the participating countries. There are some sectors, however, on which the effect will be minor or indirect. The service-producing sectors belong to this category with the exception of the transports sector and possibly commerce and banks, insurance, and financing. The goods-producing sectors, because of their very nature, will feel the effect of integration directly and with the exception of the construction subsector, will be strongly affected by it. If we consider the relative importance of a sector both in the economy and in a program of economic integration, there are two subsectors whose importance far exceeds that of the others as far as Colombia's participation in LAFTA is concerned: agriculture and livestock, and manufacturing. A somewhat detailed look at the present structure of these sectors follows.

Agriculture and Livestock

Even though its relative importance has been diminishing, the agriculture and livestock sector is still the most important in the Colombian economy. This sector accounts for nearly one-third of

TABLE 10

COLOMBIA: BALANCE OF PAYMENTS, 1961–67 (IN MILLIONS OF U.S. $)

	1961	1962	1963	1964	1965	1966	Est. 1967
Current Account							
Exports, f.o.b.	389.7[a]	394.2[a]	393.0[a]	540.9[a]	484.3[a]	468.7	442.0
Imports, f.o.b.	−530.8	−536.9	−497.5	−575.4	−423.5	−628.0	−503.0
Nonmonetary gold	14.0	13.9	11.4	12.8	11.2	9.8	9.0
Freight, net	6.0	3.7	6.3	0.5	14.6	− 12.5	27.0
Petroleum trade and services, net	28.7	28.1	13.5	5.9	22.9	15.6	11.6
Tourism, net	− 1.5	− 10.2	− 5.7	− 30.3	− 22.7	− 21.6	− 14.0
Net factor income payments to the rest of the world	− 27.9	− 36.7	− 55.9	− 73.2	− 66.3	− 74.0	− 50.0
Other, net	− 21.1	− 24.2	+ 3.1	− 30.5	− 40.8	− 19.3	− 20.0
Balance on Current Account	−142.9	−168.1	−131.8	−150.3	− 20.3	−223.1	− 97.0
Capital Account							
Central government transfers, net	7.8	8.7	9.5	9.2	7.7	− 1.0	5.0
Short-term private capital	31.0	4.1	− 13.0	69.4	−103.2	112.1	
Long-term private capital	− 20.0	21.5	71.1	98.4	38.6	40.0	17.0
Disbursements from official loans	82.7	91.0	123.4	143.9	89.7	130.0	140.0
Amortization of official loans	− 21.2	− 18.6	− 24.4	− 30.1	− 28.9	− 43.0	− 70.0
Petroleum capital transactions, net	7.6			28.4			
U.S. government holdings of Colombian pesos	1.7	0.1	3.7	4.3			
Errors and omissions, net	− 11.6[b]	− 26.0[b]	− 62.2[b]	−188.3[b]	− 49.2[b]	− 32.0	+ 45.0
Balance on Capital Account	+ 63.0	+125.0	+100.0	+135.2	+ 73.0	+168.0	+147.0
Change in Net International Reserves of the Banco de la República (−Increase)	+ 80.1	+ 43.1	+ 31.1	+ 15.1	− 53.1	+ 55.1	− 50.0

SOURCE: Organization of American States, *Domestic Exports and the Needs for External Financing for the Development of Colombia.*

a. Excludes exports of crude petroleum and fuel oil. The series 1961–65 have been adjusted in accordance with the valuation of coffee and changes in coffee stocks held abroad.

b. Includes the net changes in the international assets and liabilities of monetary sectors other than the Banco de la República.

GDP. It employs one-half of the total active population, and two of its products, coffee and bananas, generate nearly three-fourths of the country's foreign exchange.

The growth of this sector during the last decade has been less than the growth of the general economy. The trend in value of agricultural and livestock production is shown in Table 11.

Thus, the value of agricultural and livestock production has increased at an average rate of 3.0 per cent per year over the last decade, barely keeping pace with the population increase. If we consider the fact that the growth in livestock production over the period considered was almost 30 per cent greater than that of agri-

TABLE 11

INDEXES OF VALUE OF AGRICULTURE AND LIVESTOCK PRODUCTION
(INDEX 1958 = 100)

1955	89.0
1960	105.6
1961	109.6
1962	113.6
1963	113.7
1964	120.3
1965	120.5
1966	127.0
1967[a]	131.0

SOURCE: Banco de la República, *Cuentas Nacionales*, 1966.
a. Estimate by the secretariat of the Organization of American States.

cultural production,[1] we must conclude that per capita production of agricultural products has declined over the last decade in Colombia. The Colombian government is aware of this and gives very high priority to any measures tending to increase agricultural output. Price supports have been used in the past to stimulate production. Because this measure obtains results quickly, it will probably be used several times in the near future or at least until other measures that take longer to produce results have done so.

According to the last agricultural census, over 27,000,000 hectares of land were being exploited for different purposes. A breakdown of the uses of this land is shown in Table 12.

Slightly more than 18 per cent of the exploited land is classified as either arable or as permanent crops. In contrast, over 50 per

1. From figures published by Banco de la República; if 1955 was taken as a base, the indexes of value of agriculture and livestock production for 1965 would be 133.6 and 144.1, respectively.

TABLE 12

LAND USE, 1960

Use	Hectares	%
Total exploited land	27,337,827	100.0
Arable land	3,531,958	12.9
Annual crops	1,952,987	7.1
Fallow	1,578,971	5.8
Permanent crops	1,515,130	5.5
Prairies and permanent pastures	14,605,954	53.4
Forests	6,387,024	23.4
Other land	1,297,761	4.8

SOURCE: DANE, *Directorio Nacional de Explotaciones Agropecuarias, Resumen Nacional Segunda Parte.*

cent is classified as prairie and permanent pasture, which means that it is used for extensive livestock enterprises, mainly cattle.

The distribution of land according to size of holdings is shown in Table 13. Two facts are clear. First, there is a large concentration of land in the hands of a few producers since 3.6 per cent of the owners control 18 million hectares or two-thirds of the total land being used, and the top 0.6 per cent control over 40 per cent of the land. Second, at the other end of the scale, almost two-thirds of the number of holdings are smaller than 5 hectares and comprise only 4.5 per cent of the total land. For all practical purposes it can be said that all farms belonging to this latter category are subsistence farms and with very few exceptions do not belong to the marketing system. Most of the commercial agriculture takes place on the farms of 20 to 100 hectares in size. In general these are the most productive of the agricultural holdings and are where most of the ex-

TABLE 13

NUMBER AND AREA OF AGRICULTURAL HOLDINGS

Hectares	Number		Area		Average Size
	Units	%	Thous. Hectares	%	Hectares
Total	1,209,672	100.0	27,338	100.0	22.6
Less than 1	298,071	24.6	132	0.5	0.4
1 to less than 5	458,534	37.9	1,107	4.0	2.4
5 to less than 20	283,376	23.4	2,737	10.0	9.7
20 to less than 100	126,779	10.5	5,319	19.4	41.9
100 to less than 500	36,010	3.0	6,990	25.6	194.1
500 to less than 1,000	4,141	0.3	2,731	10.0	659.5
1,000 to less than 2,500	1,975	0.2	2,808	10.3	1,421.8
2,500 and over	786	0.1	5,514	20.2	7,015.3

SOURCE: DANE, *Informe al Congreso Nacional.*

port crops such as coffee and cotton are grown. They account for only 10.5 per cent of the total number of holdings and less than one-fifth of the total used acreage.

Although there are some highly modern operations, particularly in the case of corporation farming, it can be said that the level of technology of Colombian agriculture is generally low. Even though out of the 27 million hectares of land used, 18 million hectares could

TABLE 14

WORLDWIDE, TROPICAL COUNTRY, AND COLOMBIAN YIELDS, 1965
(IN KILOGRAMS PER HECTARE)

Crop	Highest Yield, All Countries		Highest Yield, Tropical Countries		Colombia
Wheat	Denmark	4,460	Mexico	2,470	900
Barley	Denmark	3,960	Kenya	1,440	1,180
Corn	Canada	4,980	Taiwan	2,200	910
Rice (paddy)	Australia	6,140	Peru	4,060	1,960
Sugarcane	Hawaii	230,000	Hawaii	230,000	41,700
Potatoes	Holland	26,200	Taiwan	13,100	7,100
Sesame	U.A.R.	1,030	Thailand	890	590
Onions	Belgium	47,300	Peru	20,800	9,700
Beans	Holland	1,930	Sudan	1,470	660
Bananas	Spain	33,900	Pakistan	30,300	15,600
Cotton seed	Israel	1,030	Honduras	1,430	710
Cotton fiber	Israel	1,230	Guatemala	840	390
Coffee	El Salvador	1,000	El Salvador	1,000	533
Cow's milk	Israel	4,902	Hawaii	4,300	279
Cattle percentage, slaughtered	Holland	40			13

SOURCE: Organization of American States, *Domestic Exports and the Needs for External Financing for the Development of Colombia.*

be mechanized, only 1,827,000 hectares were in 1964.[2] This is slightly over 10 per cent of the potential. The predominance of small farms and the scarcity of resources on the part of the farmers, as well as their lack of education and contact with the modern world, are among the causes of this low level of mechanization. According to the last agricultural census, only 28 per cent of the farms, representing slightly over 15 per cent of the total arable land, used fertilizers. The average amount of fertilizer used per hectare is, according to the same census, only about one-fourth of the recommended levels. Partly as a result of the factors mentioned above, yields in Colombia are lower in most crops than they

2. Caja de Crédito Agrario Industrial y Minero. *Mecanización Agrícola en Colombia.*

TABLE 15

AREA PLANTED FOR SELECTED CROPS, 1965

Crop	Area Planted (Hectares)
Corn	890,500
Coffee	811,400
Sugarcane	438,000
Rice	376,500
Platano	284,500
Yucca	221,000
Potatoes	170,500
Cotton	157,500
Wheat	122,900
Beans	106,300
Barley	73,200
Bananas	50,000
Cocoa	38,000
Tobacco	25,500

SOURCE: Caja de Crédito Agrario Industrial y Minero, Departamento de Investigaciones Economicas, *Mecanización Agrícola en Colombia*.

TABLE 16

LIVESTOCK INVENTORY AND SLAUGHTER, 1965

Type	Inventory (Thousands of heads)	Slaughter	Meat Production (Thousand metric tons)
Beef cattle	12,616	2,183	436.5
Dairy cattle	1,502	2,183	436.5
Dual purpose	901	2,183	436.5
Hogs	1,788	1,079	64.2
Sheep	1,702	177	3.2

SOURCE: DANE, *Encuesta Agropecuaria Nacional 1965*.

TABLE 17

FISH PRODUCTION BY ORIGIN, 1960–67 (IN THOUSAND METRIC TONS)

Year	Total	Ocean	River
1960	29.7	19.6	10.1
1961	47.5	32.4	15.1
1962	51.6	32.4	19.2
1963	47.9	25.4	22.5
1964	53.4	30.0	23.4
1965	57.0	32.3	24.7
1966	61.6	31.1	30.5
1967	65.0	33.0	32.0

SOURCE: Ministerio de Agricultura, unpublished data.

are in many countries both developed and underdeveloped. Table 14 shows a comparison of yields for selected crops in Colombia with the corresponding highest yields reported both in the world and in tropical countries. It can be observed from that table that the spread is considerable in all cases, even when comparison is made only with the tropical countries.

Table 15 shows the main crops grown in Colombia, according to area planted. With the exception of coffee, cotton, sugarcane, tobacco, and bananas, all crops are grown almost exclusively for local consumption. Special consideration will be given to these crops in chapter 5.

The livestock sector takes over 50 per cent of the total land under exploitation, and its value of production is slightly under one-half that of crop production. During the past few years this sector has been increasing in importance as a source of foreign exchange, due particularly to cattle sold alive to some Western European countries and Peru. Table 16 shows the number of head and slaughter figures for different kinds of livestock for the year 1965, the last year for which a detailed sample is available. We will take a further look at the potential of this sector in foreign trade in chapter 5.

The potential of fish as a source of foreign exchange and of proteins for the Colombian population is something that had not been studied until the late fifties and early sixties. The relative importance of fishing in the export sector will be studied in the next chapter. Table 17 shows the rate of fish production since 1960.

4. The Manufacturing Industry

T HE CHARACTERISTICS that we observe in manufacturing industry in Colombia are the result of a long-term growth process influenced by different factors. Some of these factors are associated with events that were of worldwide importance, others can be associated with conditions typical of Latin America, and finally some are connected with economic and social developments peculiar only to Colombia.

Historical Development

Previous to the twenties the industrialization efforts in Colombia had been scanty and timid. Prior to 1930 the participation of the manufacturing sector in the GDP never reached 10 per cent, and the main type of industry that existed was related to basic agricultural products, namely coffee mills and sugar refining plants. The tobacco industry had some importance as did to some extent the textile and beverage industries. The lack of foreign exchange to purchase capital goods, the low income of the population, and the lack of adequate transportation and communication facilities explain in part the industrial backwardness of the country up to 1930.

After 1930, several types of government investment took place, especially in transportation, communications, and electric energy facilities, which generated industrial activity. During those years also, foreign capital started to pour into the country, mainly from mining enterprises and certain types of services. The new customs law, introduced in 1931 with protectionist purposes, contributed to the increase in industrial activity through increased import substitution. Nevertheless, since the economy was also growing at a rapid pace, the industrialization index as represented by the percentage of manufacturing industry value in the GDP did not increase substantially. Before the beginning of World War II it was about 13 per cent,[1] and at that time the most important industries were still food processing and tobacco, although some increase in activity had taken place in the textile and cement industries.

The Second World War created a great number of difficulties in the flow of goods to Latin American countries which depended on the United States and Western Europe for the great majority of their imports. These difficulties in turn created many stimuli for developing manufacturing production. Increases in the beverage, textile, and leather articles industries were registered. For the first time large industrial establishments and the consequent large-scale production started to replace the smaller establishments. The government indirectly played a decisive role by stimulating investment, granting protection against foreign competition to newly created industry, and creating fiscal and credit incentives. It also played a direct role by investing in many types of infrastructure and by direct investment in industrial enterprises in collaboration with the private sector. The Institute of Industrial Promotion was formed in order to encourage the creation of basic industries and industries for the processing of raw materials that did not develop by private initiative alone.

Several important developments took place in the industrial structure of Colombia during the postwar years. During that period the growth of the new industries was considerably faster than the growth of the traditional ones. The chemical industry, which before the war was limited to the manufacture of candles, matches, and soap, began producing many kinds of intermediate products, drugs, and pharmaceuticals. The cement industry continued growing and received new vigor with the start of mass production of asbestos-cement products. A whole new paper and pulp products industry was born and grew. The rubber industry was developed and pro-

1. Lauchlin Currie, *Bases de un Programa de Fomento para Colombia.*

duction of many types of tires and pneumatics started. The mechanical industries advanced somewhat as did the industries derived from petroleum and coal, and the government took the initial steps toward the establishment of the first steel industry in the country. The decade of the sixties has seen the development of auto assembly plants and the birth and growth of the petrochemical industry on which a great deal of the country's industrial future may rest.

Structure of Industry

Even though the industrial structure of the country has changed somewhat since the end of World War II, the bulk of the industry still corresponds to the so-called traditional sectors. Table 18 shows that according to the industrial census of 1963, the food, beverage, tobacco, textile, and clothing industries (traditional) had 52.2 per cent of the total of industrial establishments, employed 49.3 per cent of the total industrial personnel, accounted for 46.1 per cent

TABLE 18

STRUCTURE OF INDUSTRY, 1963

Industrial Group	Number of Establishments (%)	Number of Persons (%)	Wages and Salaries Paid (%)	Value Added (%)
Food	25.6	14.4	11.8	13.8
Beverages	2.0	5.9	9.2	15.1
Tobacco	1.5	1.4	1.7	4.1
Textiles	4.1	16.1	16.5	14.9
Clothing	19.0	11.5	6.9	4.8
Wood (except furniture)	3.5	2.2	1.6	0.8
Wood furniture	3.5	1.8	1.2	1.0
Paper	0.9	2.0	2.6	2.8
Printing	4.3	4.1	4.4	2.8
Leather products	2.4	1.6	1.4	1.2
Rubber products	0.6	2.5	3.4	3.4
Chemicals	4.5	6.5	8.2	10.0
Petroleum	0.2	0.7	1.9	2.9
Nonmetallic minerals	9.4	9.0	8.7	6.1
Metallic, basic	0.3	1.2	1.3	2.7
Metallic products except machinery and transport equipment	5.9	6.6	6.3	4.5
Nonelectric machinery	2.3	1.6	1.4	1.1
Electric machinery and appliances	1.9	3.1	3.4	3.2
Transport machinery	5.5	5.0	5.4	2.5
Other manufacturing	2.6	2.8	2.7	2.3

SOURCE: DANE, *Anuario General de Estadística* (1963).

of all wages and salaries paid in industry, and in terms of value added represented 52.7 per cent of the total for industry. The same table points out the contrast that exists between the above-mentioned industries and the more modern sectors.

More important than knowledge of the present structure of industry is the change that is taking place in that structure, if any. This change can be studied by looking at the growth in value added of the different groups of the manufacturing industry as shown in Table 19. It can be observed that there are two groups that are leaders as far as growth is concerned: paper products and the mechanical industries. The clothing industry follows, reflecting the increase in urbanization mentioned before and its consequent effect on the demand for the output of this industry. Besides the ones just mentioned, only two other groups, printing and metallic basic, have grown faster than the average for all manufacturing industry. Most of the rest are either very close to or trail the general average by a few points; the leather industry shows a very slow growth rate, while the tobacco and wood products industries seem to be stagnant.

The industrial growth of Colombia shows in general terms the characteristics typical of most Latin American countries: rapid growth in sectors that are relatively new for the country, particularly in the production of intermediate goods and some light capital goods, and stagnation or slow growth in those more traditional sectors for which all the possible import substitution has been accomplished and where the size of the market hampers further expansion. Table 20 shows the annual cumulative growth of the different industries.

Number and Size of Industrial Establishments

According to the latest industrial survey of 1963, at that time the country's industry comprised 11,674 establishments. There is not a clear definition of what an "industrial establishment" as accounted for in this survey is, but judging from the fact that there are establishments included in the above number that employ one or two persons, we must conclude that the definition covers both traditional and newly established activities, small owner-operated repair shops as well as large manufacturers, units with outmoded production methods as well as others where up-to-date techniques are used. The number of establishments therefore is meaningless and of interest only as a curiosity. A better indication of the true char-

TABLE 19

GROWTH OF VALUE ADDED IN MANUFACTURING INDUSTRIES (INDEX 1958 = 100)

Industry Group	1955	1956	1957	1958	1959	1960	1961	1962	1963	1964	1965
All Groups	84	91	95	100	110	117	125	135	141	150	158
Food	94	100	96	100	109	114	123	135	128	144	159
Beverages	90	89	96	100	108	113	118	124	131	138	144
Tobacco	88	94	99	100	103	107	110	113	119	123	128
Textiles	90	91	94	100	109	119	123	131	141	148	145
Clothing	81	96	99	100	113	123	132	148	161	174	187
Wood and wood products	65	86	97	100	102	102	105	104	105	106	105
Paper	87	94	101	100	118	139	152	183	198	198	220
Printing	95	112	108	100	104	103	135	151	171	171	173
Leather	84	96	105	100	92	95	107	115	125	128	138
Rubber	80	96	99	100	105	119	128	134	137	138	141
Chemicals	80	96	95	100	116	122	129	135	141	150	157
Petroleum and coal products	62	67	82	100	104	114	124	132	128	133	145
Nonmetallic minerals	89	110	102	100	122	119	125	143	145	152	158
Metallic, basic	59	78	96	100	91	124	134	117	152	155	166
Mechanical	53	68	83	100	120	136	150	171	191	215	232

SOURCES: United Nations, Economic Commission for Latin America, *Statistical Bulletin of Latin America*, vol. 3, no. 2; Banco de la República, *Cuentas Nacionales* (1962–65).

acter of the industrial activity can be obtained from Table 21 where the total number of establishments is broken down according to number of persons employed and the percentages of certain quantities which each size class accounts for are given. It can be observed that two-thirds of the establishments covered employ less than ten persons, and their contribution to total production is only slightly over 5 per cent. The large establishments (those employing one hundred or more persons) account for only 4.2 per cent of the

TABLE 20

ANNUAL CUMULATIVE RATES OF GROWTH FOR DIFFERENT INDUSTRIES, 1958–65

Industry Group	Annual Growth (%)
Total	6.8
Traditional	
Food	6.9
Beverages	5.4
Tobacco	3.6
Textiles	5.5
Clothing	9.4
Wood and wood products	0.7
Printing	8.2
Leather	4.7
Modern	
Rubber products	5.1
Paper	11.9
Chemicals	6.7
Petroleum and coal products	5.5
Nonmetallic minerals	6.8
Metallic, basic	7.5
Mechanical	12.8

SOURCE: Calculated from the figures in Table 19.

total number, but pay two-thirds of the total wages and salaries, produce over two-thirds of the total in value terms, and account for almost three-fourths of the value added in industry.

Characteristics and Problems of Industry

The industrial sector of Colombia presents certain characteristics which are common to most Latin American countries of similar size and degree of economic development. These characteristics are a result of some of the problems that the sector has had to confront which are also common to many countries in Latin America. The most important of these characteristics probably is the high degree of protectionism that exists throughout the manufacturing industry.

Protectionism in Colombia started in the early thirties after the introduction of the new customs law. Although the law was passed as an emergency measure to deal with certain disruptions in the balance of payments and to provide revenue for the government, its effect was to encourage the local manufacture of products that were imported previously; also, the restriction of external supplies during World War II encouraged the introduction of many new industrial lines, often on very shaky foundations and with very little regard for economics. Consequently, in the subsequent years the government had to openly adopt measures in order to protect these industries from potentially fatal foreign competition. After one industry is protected it becomes extremely hard to deny the same treatment to the others. Protectionism spread and at present it is

TABLE 21

DISTRIBUTION OF ESTABLISHMENTS, WAGES AND SALARIES, VALUE
OF PRODUCTION, AND VALUE ADDED BY SIZE CLASS

Number of Persons Employed	Number of Establishments (%)	Wages and Salaries Paid (%)	Total Value of Production (%)	Value Added (%)
1–4	31.0	1.0	1.5	1.2
5–9	31.1	3.2	3.7	2.6
10–14	13.8	3.5	4.4	2.7
15–19	4.5	2.2	2.5	1.7
20–24	3.4	2.3	2.6	1.8
25–49	7.6	8.9	9.2	7.2
50–74	3.0	7.3	6.7	5.9
75–99	1.4	4.9	5.0	4.5
100–199	2.3	15.2	17.0	18.6
200 and over	1.9	51.5	47.4	53.8

SOURCE: DANE, *Anuario General de Estadística* (1963).

impossible to find an industry operating in Colombia that is not protected by import restrictions or high tariffs.

The small size of the market, already mentioned, combined with protectionism has had a threefold effect upon industry. First, it has led to the construction in some cases of small plants operating at high per unit costs, or in other cases, when entrepreneurs try to get ahead of demand, of large plants which operate well below capacity with the consequent waste of scarce capital. Second, it has led to the creation of several multiproduct plants. Finally, it has led to the construction of inefficiently integrated plants producing parts of a product as well as the completed product. The second and third types of plants imply a loss in productivity by not being able to take advantage of specialization. The result, then, has been not only inefficient levels of production but also the encouragement of undesirable horizontal and vertical integration.

Colombian industry confronts two other problems which should be mentioned here. First, there is a shortage of capital which is compounded by the fact that most firms are forced to use a high proportion for working capital in order to keep up large stocks of raw materials and goods and to grant sizeable volumes of credit in order to sell their products. Second, there is the high dependency on imported raw materials which makes industrial activity dependent on the balance of payments situation.

Competitiveness of Colombian Industry

Because of the above, costs of production and prices of manufactured goods in Colombia are high compared to those in more developed economies. Although this is a fact that is generally recognized, there are no quantitative studies on the factors determining those price levels, that is, how far they may be influenced by relatively high production costs or gross rates of return, distribution and marketing margins, indirect taxes on transactions or consumption, customs duties and other equivalent charges in imports, et cetera. This is a highly complex area of study and a very important and necessary one. A study along these lines is a basic need for determining the position of the country within an integrated Latin America and the effect that many integration clauses and measures could have upon this position.

The only bases for determining the relative position of Colombian industry vis-à-vis other LAFTA countries are some comparisons, made by the Economic Commission for Latin America, of unit prices of certain manufactured products. The unit prices of some products which are either manufactured or assembled in Colombia were selected and translated into index numbers; they are shown in Table 22. Before the data in this table are analyzed some words of caution are necessary. First, since some of the products are not manufactured in all countries the index numbers here may reflect customs duties more than anything else; the same can be said of those products assembled in the country but with imported inputs. This is particularly true in the case of consumer durables and household appliances. Second, the prices at which some products are sold in the home market may very well be quite different from the prices charged to export markets and some firms will, as some already have, use price discrimination. Third, the figures are affected by the fact that some currencies may have been overvalued while others may have been undervalued at the time the comparison was made.

The first thing that Table 22 shows is that, typically, prices in the LAFTA countries are considerably higher than in the United States. Since most countries do a great proportion of their trade with the United States, this is an obstacle to integration. Very strong arguments will have to be used before imports from other LAFTA countries substitute for imports from the United States.

TABLE 22

COMPARISON OF UNIT PRICES OF CERTAIN MANUFACTURED PRODUCTS, 1962

Product	Colombia	Argentina	Brazil	Chile	Peru	Mexico	Venezuela	United States
Household soap	100	82	79	197	158	145	167	150
Vitamin C	100	360	60	80	100	50	400	50
Penicillin	100	137	57	57	71	63	148	80
Cotton fabrics	100	140	170	220	200	80	130	60
Rayon fabrics	100	228	200	243	257	200	114	86
Woollen fabrics	100	129	471	107	114	143	107	114
Cement	100	200	167	100	133	133	67	100
Electric bulbs	100	100	150	80	90	64	36	54
Refrigerators	100	93	96	253	133	133	40	24
Washing machines	100	75	91	132	76	103	59	34
Sewing machines	100	80	100	68	96	104	56	42
Radio sets	100	161	177	200	161	185	62	46
T.V. sets	100	67	89	167	56	56	44	11
Typewriters	100	110	152	176	130	108	45	70
Electric motors	100	64	50	105	84	105	36	47

SOURCE: Calculated from figures given in United Nations, Economic Commission for Latin America, *The Process of Industrial Development of Latin America*. Comparisons based on estimated parity exchange rates.

The two pharmaceutical products listed, vitamin C capsules and penicillin, can apparently be produced more cheaply in at least three other LAFTA countries. The difference in price appears to be substantial and it would seem that not even high transportation costs could overcome the advantage. In the field of textiles, Colombia undersells all the other LAFTA countries. This has been proved in some studies, and it is in this field where Colombian know-how and productivity are greater.[2] However, it must be remembered that because of the nature of this industry, all countries in the re-

2. See for example United Nations, Economic Commission for Latin America, *The Process of Industrial Development of Latin America*, pp. 92–97.

gion are engaged in it and protectionist pressures will be sure to arise if inclusion of textiles in the Common List were proposed.

The price of cement is also lower in Colombia than in any other LAFTA country with the exception of Venezuela. This advantage has been translated into exports not only of cement but of some manufactured products which use cement as an important input as will be shown in the following chapters.

In the field of household appliances and certain consumer durables, two things can be observed: for typewriters and radio sets Colombia undersells all countries listed with the exception of Venezuela; however, for the major appliances (refrigerators, washing machines, sewing machines, and television sets), Argentina, Brazil, and Venezuela produce at lower prices. This should be expected due to the larger market size in the cases of Argentina and Brazil and to the imports of inputs with practically no custom duties in Venezuela. With respect to electric motors only Chile and Mexico show prices higher than Colombia.

All the structural defects that have been pointed out concerning Colombian industry are present in the majority of the LAFTA countries and in many cases to a greater extent. Thus, although it would be almost impossible for Colombian industry to compete with more developed nations under the present circumstances, it can successfully confront other countries in the area which are at a similar or lower state of economic development. The trade figures with some of the LAFTA countries, which will be analyzed later, seem to confirm this opinion.

5. The Foreign Trade of Colombia

T HE LACK of dynamism shown by the export sector of the Colombian economy from the mid-fifties to mid-sixties is one of
the main bottlenecks that the country faces and is a great obstacle to its economic development. Since exports are the main
source of foreign exchange needed to finance the country's growing
needs of productive equipment, the long-run improvement in the
standard of living of the Colombian people is closely related to the
balance of trade situation. In order to make a realistic appraisal of
the country's future position within LAFTA it is necessary to analyze
the evolution and main characteristics of the export sector.

Growth Rate of Exports

The figures in Table 23 do not present a very encouraging picture. Total exports show a fluctuating pattern with a tendency to
remain constant around the $500 million figure, having always been
above $400 million (except in 1950) and reaching a peak of $657
million in 1954. It is fairly obvious that the great expansion in
world trade that has taken place since the end of World War II
has not been shared by Colombia. Furthermore, the proportion of
Colombian exports relative to total world exports has declined from
around 0.75 per cent in 1953 to less than 0.3 per cent in 1966. Thus,

while world exports have more than doubled in value over the last fifteen years, and those of the less developed nations have increased in absolute terms but decreased relative to the total, Colombian exports have remained constant in absolute terms and deteriorated in relative terms—a very unfavorable situation indeed.

Structure of Exports

The composition of Colombian exports shows the characteristics typical of the less developed countries, namely very high dependency on one product, a high percentage of agricultural products

TABLE 23

TOTAL VALUE OF EXPORTS, 1950–67

Year	F.O.B. Value (Million U.S. $)
1950	395.6
1951	463.3
1952	473.3
1953	596.1
1954	657.1
1955	583.9
1956	537.0
1957	511.1
1958	460.7
1959	473.0
1960	464.6
1961	434.5
1962	463.4
1963	446.7
1964	548.1
1965	539.1
1966	507.7
1967	509.9

SOURCE: DANE, *Anuario de Comercio Exterior,* several issues, and *Boletín Mensual de Estadística,* several issues.

and raw materials, a low percentage of manufactured goods, and erratic or fluctuating patterns in some other products (cotton, sugar).

The export picture has been dominated by one agricultural commodity: coffee. Although the importance of this product as a source of foreign exchange has diminished considerably over the last decade, it still accounts for over two-thirds of the total value of Colombian exports. Next in importance is crude petroleum, which in 1966 accounted for 14.1 per cent of total value.

In the Colombian foreign trade language, all exports except

coffee and crude oil are known as *exportaciones menores* or minor exports. In an effort to diminish the dependence on coffee and oil, the Colombian government gives special incentives and foreign exchange privileges to the exporters of the so-called minor exports. These measures have been effective insofar as the percentage composition of exports has evolved in favor of the minor exports (see Table 24). The growth of this latter group both in absolute and relative terms has been particularly significant in the last three years, but this is too short a time to know whether it is a sporadic phenomenon or an indication of a trend that will continue into the future. This growth has two components worth mentioning: first, the growth in certain exports that might be called traditional since they are raw commodities and have occupied a rather important

TABLE 24

EVOLUTION OF MAJOR AND MINOR EXPORTS, 1961–67

Year	Major Exports		Minor Exports	
	Value (Million $)	%	Value (Million $)	%
1961	376.1	86.5	58.4	13.5
1962	392.6	84.7	70.8	15.3
1963	380.2	85.1	66.5	14.9
1964	469.2	85.6	78.9	14.4
1965	432.0	80.1	107.1	19.9
1966	400.0	78.8	107.6	21.2
1967	383.6	75.2	126.3	24.8

SOURCE: Calculated from figures published in DANE, *Anuario de Comercio Exterior* and *Boletín Mensual de Estadística,* several issues.

place in the export picture for quite some time. These are fuel oil, bananas, leaf tobacco, and sugar. The value of exports of these commodities increased from $28.1 million in 1961 to $43.6 million in 1966 or at a rate of over 9 per cent per year.

The second factor contributing to the increase in minor exports was the growth of the category classified as "others" (Table 25). This category, in which all the very small items and those of sporadic appearance in the export lists are grouped, accounted for only 3.7 per cent of total trade in 1961. However, by 1966 it accounted for 16.7 per cent of total exports. This has been accomplished in part by the growth in exports of some items like beef, vegetable cakes, cotton yarn, and textiles, and in part by the addition of new items, most of them light manufactures. The importance that the "others" category has acquired over the last three years demands a more detailed breakdown. The values of exports of the most important products in this category for 1965 and 1966 are shown in Table 26. Also included in the table are those items whose value in either year was over $1 million; in 1966 they represented about two-thirds of the total value of the "others" group.

The opening of new lines of trade and the consequent increase of exports other than the traditional coffee and petroleum are healthy signs. However, there is still much to be done since the 1966 figures show that *less than 10 per cent* of total exports was accounted for by items with any degree of manufacture.

TABLE 25

Main Exports, 1961–66 (Million $)

Commodity	1961	1962	1963	1964	1965	1966
Total	434.5	463.4	446.7	548.1	539.1	507.6
Coffee	307.8	332.0	303.0	394.2	343.9	328.3
Crude oil	68.2	60.6	77.2	75.0	88.2	71.7
Fuel oil	4.8	7.1	3.8	7.3	7.3	9.7
Bananas	14.1	10.6	13.3	12.4	18.6	20.0
Leaf tobacco	4.0	5.7	7.2	9.4	7.2	5.6
Raw cotton	10.1	15.6	9.3	6.3	8.0	2.2
Sugar	5.2	7.4	5.5	3.3	7.6	8.3
Naphthenic acid	0.6	0.1	0.3	0.3	0.3	0.3
Shrimp	1.4	1.5	1.4	1.0	1.4	1.1
Cement	2.4	2.0	1.6	1.9	2.0	2.1
Lumber	2.2	2.2	2.8	3.9	3.2	2.9
Grain mills	0.6	0.6	0.6	0.8	0.7	0.4
Platinum	1.5	1.0	1.6	1.5	0.9	
Others	11.6	17.0	19.1	30.8	49.8	55.0

Source: DANE, *Anuario de Comercio Exterior*, several issues.

Geographic Destination of Exports

As important as the evolution of the value and structure of exports are the geographical changes that take place in them and the relative importance of different countries and regions as buyers of Colombian products. From Table 27 it can be seen that the United States is by far the most important buyer of Colombian exports. However, its relative importance has declined considerably. Although in 1960, 65.4 per cent of all Colombian exports went to the United States, this percentage was reduced to 43.4 in 1966. This was due in part to increasing sales to the European Economic Community (EEC), which in 1966 absorbed 24.0 per cent of all Colom-

TABLE 26

VALUE OF EXPORTS OF SELECTED PRODUCTS INCLUDED IN THE CATEGORY
"OTHERS," 1965–66

Item	F.O.B. Value (Thousand $)	
	1965	1966
Beef cattle	6,344	5,998
Paper and cardboard containers	83	5,716
Cotton textiles	5,809	4,118
Automobile tires	2,172	3,878
Leather goods, skins, hides	4,429	3,640
Cotton yarn	3,159	2,966
Vegetable cakes	2,313	2,705
Liquid ammonia	2,249	2,587
Cement tubes	157	1,623
Beef (fresh, frozen, chilled)	2,435	1,363
Medicines	1,151	1,311

SOURCE: DANE, *Anuario de Comercio Exterior* (1966).

bian exports compared with 18.2 per cent in 1960. The EEC is the second important buyer of Colombian products. Exports to the countries of LAFTA also increased during the sixties, going from 1.6 per cent to 7.3 per cent. Of great significance also is the increased importance of the "rest of the world" which doubled its participation from 1960 to 1966. The gain in this category was partially due to increased sales to the Eastern European countries (East Germany, Czechoslovakia, Hungary, Poland, and Rumania). Exports to these countries increased from slightly under $1 million in 1960 to more than $15.9 million in 1966. Exports to Spain and Yugo-

TABLE 27

GEOGRAPHIC DESTINATION OF EXPORTS, 1960–66 (IN PER CENT)

Economic Area	1960	1961	1962	1963	1964	1965	1966
Total	100.0	100.0	100.0	100.0	100.0	100.0	100.0
United States	65.4	62.9	59.3	56.4	54.0	47.6	43.4
European Economic Community	18.2	19.0	19.9	21.2	23.1	24.2	24.0
European Free Trade Association	6.3	7.6	7.9	7.4	7.6	7.7	7.5
Latin American Free Trade Association	1.6	2.0	2.1	1.8	2.7	4.2	7.3
Central American Common Market	0.1	0.4	0.4	0.8	0.9	1.4	0.9
Rest of the world	8.4	8.1	10.4	12.4	11.7	14.9	16.9

SOURCE: Calculated from figures published in several issues of DANE, *Boletín Mensual de Estadística.*

slavia went from $6 million to $22 million during the same period of time.

The European Free Trade Association buys around 7 per cent of Colombian exports, but its relative importance has remained stable over the last six years. The participation of the Central American Common Market is negligible, but increasing.

Since the prime interest of this study is to investigate the potential for trade with the LAFTA countries, an analysis of this trade, country by country, will be made in the next chapter. In this chapter, the analysis will be limited to the principal exports and their destinations during the last two years for which data are available. The figures are shown in Table 28.

Coffee.—This has traditionally been the most important Colombian export. The United States is still the largest importer followed by West Germany, but new markets have been opened over the last few years particularly among the countries of the European Free Association and East Germany. There are only three countries in LAFTA, Argentina, Chile, and Uruguay, that buy Colombian coffee. Sales to Argentina have been developed over the last five years. Previous to that Brazil was the only supplier. Meanwhile, sales to Chile and Uruguay have dropped considerably.

Crude Petroleum and Fuel Oil.—Traditionally, the United States and Britain have been the main importers of crude petroleum usually accounting for over 50 per cent of the total sales of this product. Puerto Rico is a sporadic buyer and in 1965 imported over $28 million worth of crude oil. Trinidad and Tobago have figured as important customers on several occasions, sometimes with over $30 million imported. The United States is the main buyer of fuel oil, followed by Peru, which imported $1.6 and $2.3 million worth in 1965 and 1966, respectively. The petroleum industry is a highly sensitive one in Latin America and because of its strategic importance is always subject to a high degree of political interference. Just recently the LAFTA negotiations were stalled after an attempt to include petroleum on the Common List. The prospects for developing a stable market for petroleum and its products within the region are rather dim.

Bananas.—West Germany, the Netherlands, Sweden, and Italy accounted for 100 per cent and 94 per cent of all the exports of this commodity during 1965 and 1966, respectively. Colombia, Brazil, and Ecuador produce considerable amounts of bananas, and intra-LAFTA trade has been limited to small quantities flowing mainly

TABLE 28

EXPORTS OF IMPORTANT ITEMS AND MAIN COUNTRIES OF DESTINATION, 1965–66

Item, Countries	Value of Exports (Million $)		Item, Countries		
	1965	1966		1965	1966
Coffee			Cotton Textiles		
United States	185.5	160.4	United States	3.2	2.3
West Germany	49.2	53.9	Canada	.7	.8
Spain	18.2	19.1	Automobile Tires		
Sweden	18.3	15.9	Argentina	2.1	3.6
Finland	9.4	12.1	Leather Goods		
Netherlands	14.8	11.7	United States	1.8	1.9
East Germany	4.8	7.2	Japan	.4	.3
Belgium and			Lumber		
Luxembourg	8.6	5.9	United States	1.8	2.1
Argentina	2.2	5.5	Canada	.5	.4
Canada	7.2	4.6	United Kingdom	.3	.3
Crude Petroleum			Vegetable Cakes		
United States	34.2	29.6	Belgium and		
Trinidad and Tobago	.9	21.6	Luxembourg	.7	1.0
United Kingdom	13.9	14.8	Netherlands	1.0	.4
Spain	4.7	3.8	Cotton Yarn		
Puerto Rico	28.2	.9	United States	1.2	1.2
Netherlands	4.2	.4	Canada	.7	1.2
Bananas			Portland Cement		
West Germany	9.7	8.4	Puerto Rico	1.0	.9
Netherlands	6.4	7.1	Brazil	.1	.4
Sweden	1.9	1.9	Liquid Ammonia		
Italy	.6	1.4	United States	.7	2.2
Fuel Oil			Costa Rica	1.5	.4
United States	4.2	5.6	Shrimp		
Peru	1.6	2.3	United States	1.4	1.1
Sugar			Medicines		
United States	6.8	7.5	Ecuador	.7	.8
United Kingdom		0.8	Cement Tubes		
Beef Cattle (sold alive)			Ecuador	.3	1.0
Peru	1.9	5.2	Venezuela	.2	.6
West Germany		0.8	Beef, (fresh, frozen,		
Italy	3.9		and chilled)		
Tobacco			Spain	1.3	.4
West Germany	1.7	1.5	Peru	.1	.4
Spain	.3	1.4	France	.5	
United States	2.0	.8			

SOURCE: DANE, *Boletín Mensual de Estadística* (Mar., 1967).

from Ecuador to Chile and from Brazil to Argentina, the latter flow tending to disappear.

Sugar.—All the exports of this commodity go to the United States and the United Kingdom. Most LAFTA countries are self-sufficient in this product and only Venezuela appears as a prospective buyer of sugar. Chile, the only importer, has substituted Peruvian sugar for Colombian.

Beef Cattle.—The export of live beef cattle is of relatively recent occurrence and the Cattle Federation is in the process of developing markets, particularly in Europe. In 1965, Italy and Peru were the main buyers, and in 1966 all exports went to Peru and West Germany, with Peru absorbing $5.2 million worth or almost 80 per cent of the total value. The lack of experience and knowledge of marketing techniques caused the delivery of cattle to Italy to be unsatisfactory to the importers and no more sales have been made there. Peru, however, seems to be interested in a long-term contract for delivering live cattle for slaughtering locally. Since transportation to Peru is much less complicated than to Europe, and since local production is not increasing fast enough to guarantee satisfaction of both the Peruvian and European demands in the near future, it seems probable that sales will be concentrated on Peru in the next few years. This seems to be a good export prospect within LAFTA.

Tobacco.—West Germany, Spain, and the United States are the main importers of tobacco. Uruguay is the only country in LAFTA that buys any Colombian tobacco, and the value of its purchases is usually in the neighborhood of $100,000 and does not seem to be increasing.

Cotton Textiles and Yarn.—The bulk of the sales of these products goes to the United States and Canada with some small amounts going to Panama, Nicaragua, Peru, and Ecuador. The last two, which are LAFTA members, have each purchased an average of $120,000 per year over the last two years. As mentioned before, all countries in LAFTA have well-established if not efficient textile industries and exports to them can be expected to be sporadic and limited to some specialty types of material. Value of sales should not be expected to be much higher than what the statistics show so far.

Automobile Tires.—This is a relatively new export item. Over 90 per cent of the total goes to Argentina with very small amounts going to Paraguay and Peru. Since this is not a negotiated product it is difficult to foresee whether exports will continue at the present level.

Leather Goods.—The United States and Japan are the main importers. The possibilities of exports of these items to LAFTA are very slim.

Lumber.—The United States, Canada, and the United Kingdom buy almost all of Colombia's lumber exports. Sale of some precious woods to Mexico has taken place since 1965.

Cement and Cement Products.—Most of the sales of Portland cement have been to Puerto Rico and Brazil. Peru has occasionally imported some minor amounts. In 1966 Peru's imports were valued at $200,000. Ecuador and Venezuela imported cement tubes for a value of $1.6 million in 1966, and preliminary data indicate that this figure will easily be doubled in 1967. Colombia seems to be able to produce cement and its products cheaper than any other LAFTA country, and therefore the prospects within LAFTA for this line of exports are good.

Liquid Ammonia.—The United States is the main importer of liquid ammonia followed by Costa Rica which has purchased almost $2 million worth during 1965–66. Peru and Chile imported some Colombian ammonia in 1961 but since then their imports have stopped. The possibility of reopening these markets should be studied.

Shrimp.—Exports of shrimp go exclusively to the United States. Although there are indications that exports of this product could be tripled in the near future, the entire increase will probably be absorbed by the United States.[1] Local production satisfies local demand for shrimp in most LAFTA countries, and since it is considered a rather sumptuous commodity, prospects for trade expansion within the region are very slim.

In the preceding paragraphs, the geographic destinations of the main items whose export value during either 1965 or 1966 was $1 million or more have been examined. The importance of these products is further proven if we consider that during 1965 and 1966 they accounted for 95 per cent of the total value of exports. It can be said that these products constitute the core of the Colombian exports sector and represent some of the industries in which the country seems to enjoy certain comparative advantage. It is interesting to notice the following facts about these exports. (1) The United States is the principal importer of eleven of these products, and fifteen are sold mainly to either the United States or Western Europe. (2) There were eight products which were exported to countries belonging to LAFTA. For only five of these did the value of sales to a single country exceed $1 million in 1966, and of the five only two were manufactures: automobile tires sold to Argentina and cement tubes sold to Ecuador.

1. *Plan Nacional de Pesca.*

Volume of Imports

Due to the economic structure of the country, the volume of imports has always been dependent on the fluctuations of the purchasing power of the two main export commodities, coffee and petroleum, as well as on the movements registered in the capital account of the balance of payments. Due to the highly volatile nature of world prices of primary commodities, the erratic pattern shown by the total value of imports in Table 29 should not come as a surprise.

TABLE 29

VALUE OF IMPORTS, 1950–67

Year	C.I.F. Value of Imports (Million $)
1950	364.7
1951	419.0
1952	415.4
1953	546.7
1954	671.8
1955	669.3
1956	657.2
1957	482.6
1958	399.9
1959	415.6
1960	518.6
1961	557.1
1962	540.4
1963	506.0
1964	586.3
1965	453.5
1966	674.3
1967[a]	496.9

SOURCE: DANE, *Anuario de Comercio Exterior,* several issues.
a. Estimates.

The value has fluctuated between $365 and $674 million during the period 1950–67, and no clear trend is shown. If the averages of the first and last five years are taken we observe an average growth rate of 1.7 per cent per year which is mainly due to the fact that 1950 was the year of lowest imports during the period. However, if the average of 1951–55 is taken as the initial period instead, a slight decrease from $544.4 to $543.4 million can be observed. Thus, it can be said that the general level of imports has remained practically unchanged over the last two decades.

Structure of Imports

Although the total value of imports has remained rather stagnant, the change in the structure of those imports has been significant. The first thing to be observed in Table 30, which shows the structure of imports from 1960 to 1966, is the decline in absolute as well as relative terms of the imports of consumer goods—the increase shown in 1966 was due to the momentary opening of automobile imports which had been highly restricted since 1961 and which

TABLE 30

STRUCTURE OF IMPORTS, 1960–66

	1960	1961	1962	1963	1964	1965	1966
	C.I.F. Value (Million $)						
Total	518.6	557.1	540.4	506.0	586.3	453.5	674.3
Consumer Goods	36.4	59.4	34.2	28.2	29.0	21.0	41.9
Nondurable	17.1	19.2	15.2	13.8	10.5	6.4	13.7
Durable	19.3	40.2	19.0	14.4	18.5	14.6	28.2
Intermediate Goods	240.5	262.5	263.1	256.5	288.7	182.3	306.2
Raw materials	31.6	44.3	41.1	35.8	46.9	44.0	58.8
Semimanufactured and manufactured goods	208.9	218.2	222.0	220.7	241.8	138.3	247.4
Capital Goods	167.2	170.1	175.1	158.0	196.5	177.2	198.2
Nonclassified Articles	74.5	65.1	68.0	63.3	72.1	73.0	128.0
	Percentages						
Consumer Goods	7.0	10.7	6.3	5.6	5.0	4.6	6.2
Nondurable	3.3	3.5	2.8	2.7	1.8	1.4	2.0
Durable	3.7	7.2	3.5	2.9	3.2	3.2	4.2
Intermediate Goods	46.4	47.1	48.7	50.7	49.2	40.2	45.4
Raw materials	6.1	8.0	7.6	7.1	8.0	9.7	8.7
Semimanufactured and manufactured goods	40.3	39.1	41.1	43.6	41.2	30.5	36.7
Capital Goods	32.2	30.5	32.4	31.2	33.5	39.1	29.4
Nonclassified Articles	14.4	11.7	12.6	12.5	12.3	16.1	19.0

SOURCE: DANE, *Boletín Mensual de Estadística*, several issues.

were closed again by the end of 1966. Although not shown in the table, this category (consumer goods) accounted for 20 per cent of total imports during the early fifties[2] while presently it is of the order of 5 per cent. Within this category the decline has been faster in the subgroup "nondurables" than in the "durables." This is to be expected due to the industrialization and import substitution processes that are taking place in Colombia and which are typical of most developing nations.

2. United Nations, *Economic Survey of Latin America.*

Intermediate goods take the largest share of the total value of imports, fluctuating between 40 and 50 per cent during the years shown in the table, and show neither an increasing nor decreasing tendency. The rigidity of this group is due on the one hand to the failure of the country to augment its exports and consequently its purchasing power, thus putting an upper limit on imports, and, on the other hand, to the fact that any reduction in imports of intermediate goods affects not only the level of consumption but also directly the level of employment, which puts a lower bound on this type of import. Within this category, it can be observed that there is an increasing participation of raw materials while the importance of manufactured and semimanufactured products is somewhat diminishing—this is a further indication of the industrialization process.

Finally, the capital goods category shows the most irregularities. The sharp fluctuations that occur in this group are to be expected since by its own nature it is the most elastic of the three, and therefore it tends to reflect more the fluctuations in foreign exchange availability.

Table 31 lists the principal items imported between 1961 and 1966. An analysis of the products that are important in the trade with other LAFTA countries will be made in the next chapter and therefore a detailed analysis of this table is not necessary here. It will be sufficient to point out the following general highlights. (1) Among the raw material imports, wheat, raw cacao, raw wool, and long staple cotton have steadily increased in value while natural rubber has shown a tendency to remain constant (synthetic rubber on the other hand has more than doubled its value over the period). Imports of copra oil have decreased by over 50 per cent due to local production of substitutes. (2) In the semimanufactured and manufactured subgroup of intermediate goods, it is interesting to note the importance that chemical fertilizers still have ($13.8 million in 1966); imports of newspaper continue to be a burden on the trade balance. Wood paste imports keep soaring, and the products used in the chemical and pharmaceutical industries continue to be very important.

To summarize, the present import structure of Colombia shows the typical characteristics of a developing nation: a high degree of self-sufficiency in most consumer goods (low imports); high dependency on imports of intermediate goods and therefore a level of employment that is very vulnerable to changes in the capacity

TABLE 31

Main Import Items, 1961–66 (C.I.F. Value, Million $)

Item	1961	1962	1963	1964	1965	1966
Agricultural tractors	7.9	7.5	7.7	8.9	7.5	7.4
Aircraft	11.5	1.9	1.2	3.5	7.1	6.4
Antibiotics, pure form	3.9	3.3	5.3	5.1	3.1	4.3
Anticryptogam preparations, disinfectants, insecticides, etc.	10.3	7.2	7.0	3.4	4.1	
Artificial resins, in blades	4.2	4.7	6.3	8.1	4.2	
Automobiles	24.1	3.5	1.4	2.8	4.2	18.1
Cacao, raw	3.8	4.6	3.6	6.1	7.0	8.4
Cellulose derivatives, in powder	3.1	1.7	2.8	4.2	4.0	
Centrifugal and other types of pumps	3.1	4.0	3.2	4.1	3.8	5.8
Chemical fertilizers	13.2	13.4	8.6	10.8	4.3	13.8
Coloring materials derived from coal tar	3.3	3.3	4.6	4.5	2.6	8.1
Copra	5.9	5.1	2.7	3.4	1.2	2.7
Cordage for manufacture of tires	1.8	3.6	3.4	3.4	4.2	4.1
Cotton	0.3	0.4	1.2	2.1	5.6	4.1
Denatured tallow	2.7	3.4	3.5	5.0	5.6	9.2
Diesel-electric locomotives	2.8	0.3	4.4	1.3		
Electric generators	8.9	4.3	6.2	4.6	5.5	3.9
Electric transformers	3.3	3.8	3.0	4.5	2.8	2.4
Electrical apparatus for telephone work	4.1	6.5	6.5	8.7	8.2	8.4
Internal combustion engines and parts	19.1	21.8	23.6	25.1	11.7	19.6
Iron and steel pipes and tubes	7.3	7.0	10.2	11.1	4.9	5.7
Iron and steel sheets	19.9	19.1	18.1	21.2	13.9	
Jeeps	7.5	6.3	2.6	3.8	4.6	7.7
Lubricating oils	7.0	7.5	6.3	3.0	1.4	0.7
Metal-working machinery and tools	7.0	5.9	5.1	7.2	10.6	0.3
Moving and handling machinery	8.9	9.3	7.3	7.9	6.7	5.5
Newsprint	6.2	7.9	6.7	6.8	7.4	7.7
Other parts for automotive vehicles	3.5	4.0	4.6	4.8	2.5	7.7
Parts for automotive transmissions	6.6	7.5	10.1	10.9	4.2	7.7
Paraffin	4.0	3.4	3.6	4.1	2.9	4.3
Parts for tractors	6.0	4.4	4.5	6.1	2.1	2.7
Rubber, natural	3.3	4.7	4.6	3.3	3.9	5.5
Rubber, synthetic	3.0	4.0	4.6	4.1	4.6	6.2
Trucks and pick-ups	4.7	4.8	11.7	9.8	11.0	16.5
Wheat	11.3	13.0	8.3	12.8	12.9	20.1
Wood paste (cellulose)	4.9	6.0	7.1	7.0	7.8	10.0
Wool, raw	2.1	6.3	8.3	10.5	7.9	8.2

Source: dane, *Anuario de Comercio Exterior*, several issues.

to import; and finally a close relationship between the availability of foreign exchange and the imports of capital goods which means that the former affects the investment level and consequently the rate of development.

Origin of Imports

With the exception of the European Economic Community, whose importance as a supplier shows a declining tendency instead of an increasing one, the geographic distribution and evolution of imports are almost identical to those of exports previously discussed. The main features are a very large but decreasing importance of the United States, a tendency of imports from the European Free Trade Association to remain constant, an increasing importance of the Latin American Free Trade Association, and negligible par-

TABLE 32

GEOGRAPHIC ORIGIN OF IMPORTS, 1960–66 (IN PER CENT)

Economic Area	1960	1961	1962	1963	1964	1965	1966
Total	100.0	100.0	100.0	100.0	100.0	100.0	100.0
United States	57.1	51.6	52.4	51.9	48.3	47.8	48.0
European Economic Community	18.9	20.9	19.4	18.2	18.4	17.1	18.6
European Free Trade Assoc.	11.1	12.3	12.3	10.4	11.3	10.0	10.0
Latin American Free Trade Assoc.	1.6	2.2	2.6	4.5	6.0	8.7	8.6
Central American Common Market	0.3	0.2	0.4	0.1	0.1	0.1	0.1
Rest of the world	11.0	12.8	12.9	14.9	15.9	16.3	14.7

SOURCE: DANE, *Boletín Mensual de Estadística*, several issues.

ticipation of the Central American Common Market. Imports from the rest of the world, like exports, also showed an increase in relative importance. The percentages accounted for by the different economic areas are shown in Table 32. The next chapter will deal in detail with the trade of Colombia with LAFTA.

6. Colombia's Trade with LAFTA

ETWEEN 1962, the year in which the Montevideo Treaty started to take effect, and 1967, total intraregional trade of LAFTA increased from $774.4 to $1,428.2 million (Table 33), or at a rate of 13.0 per cent per year.

During the same period of time, the total value of exports of the LAFTA countries increased from $5.20 to $6.87 billion while the total value of their imports increased from $5.98 to $6.91 billion (Table 34). Again, in terms of cumulative annual rates this represents an increase in total exports of 5.7 per cent per year and an increase in total imports of 3.0 per cent per year.

Comparison of the above rates indicates that intraregional commerce has been a dynamic element in the foreign trade of the region. However, a look at the total trade figures shows that the importance of intraregional trade remains rather low (10.4 per cent of total trade in 1967 compared with 6.9 per cent in 1962), and that its rate of increase is getting lower; in 1967 there was actually a decline in the value of total trade.

Due to the small importance of intraregional with respect to total trade it appears difficult to determine to what extent trade with LAFTA members has substituted for trade with other countries. This could only be done after a product by product, country by

TABLE 33

EVOLUTION OF TOTAL INTRA-LAFTA[a] TRADE (IN MILLION $)

Year	Exports	Imports	Total Trade
1957–61 average	345.8	386.3	732.1
1962	354.3	420.1	774.4
1963	425.2	525.1	950.3
1964	557.6	645.7	1,203.3
1965	635.2	768.1	1,403.3
1966	695.8	806.5	1,502.3
1967[b]	662.0	766.2	1,428.2

SOURCE: LAFTA, *ALALC Síntesis Mensual* (Apr., 1967; Feb., 1968).

a. Venezuela and Bolivia are not included in any LAFTA statistics prior to 1968.

b. Figures for Chile were estimated on the basis of data for the first nine months.

country analysis. However, the difference between the rates of growth of total imports and total exports indicates that the intra-regional share of total imports has increased faster than the intra-regional share of total exports. Thus, it might be theorized that if such substitution has taken place for the region as a whole, it has been more significant in imports than in exports. In other words, it might be said that in general the countries have found it easier to look at the region as a supplier of goods that were previously imported from outside than as a market for commodities that had other outlets before. This is a logical consequence of the fact that most LAFTA countries are exporters of a limited number of primary commodities while the bulk of their imports consists of many different intermediate products.

Aggregate figures like those in Tables 33 and 34 give general indications about trends for the region as a whole, but they show

TABLE 34

EVOLUTION OF TOTAL TRADE OF LAFTA[a] COUNTRIES (IN MILLION $)

Year	Exports	Imports	Total Trade
1962	5,204.6	5,978.1	11,182.7
1963	5,621.7	5,667.7	11,289.4
1964	6,099.1	5,976.3	12,075.4
1965	6,526.9	5,989.2	12,516.1
1966	7,102.1	6,816.6	13,918.7
1967	6,865.5	6,910.7	13,776.2

SOURCE: Calculated from the figures published in International Monetary Fund, *International Financial Statistics*.

a. Venezuela and Bolivia not included.

nothing concerning the relative position of the different countries. In order to analyze the position of one or several countries vis-à-vis the other partners, a breakdown of the data is necessary. This will be done in the following section.

Country Structure of Regional Trade

Table 35 shows the relative importance of each country, and the evolution of its importance, in intra-LAFTA trade from 1962 to 1967. The first column of figures indicates the importance for the five-year period 1957–61 and is included for comparative purposes. By total trade is meant the sum of the values of imports and exports,

TABLE 35

Distribution of Intra-LAFTA Trade (Percentages of Total Trade)

Country	1957–61 Average	1962	1963	1964	1965	1966	1967
Total	100.0	100.0	100.0	100.0	100.0	100.0	100.0
Colombia	1.9	2.7	2.9	3.7	3.6	8.5	4.3
Argentina	36.7	31.6	30.2	32.4	34.7	31.2	33.8
Brazil	28.2	26.4	25.2	25.0	27.6	23.2	22.8
Chile	13.8	15.4	17.8	15.2	12.5	13.0	15.7
Ecuador	1.3	1.3	1.4	1.6	1.7	1.4	1.9
Mexico	1.2	2.9	2.9	4.3	4.7	6.0	6.0
Paraguay	2.7	2.2	2.0	2.2	2.2	2.3	2.3
Peru	8.8	12.1	11.7	10.3	9.6	9.6	8.9
Uruguay	5.4	5.4	4.9	5.3	3.4	4.8	4.3

SOURCE: Calculated from the figures in Tables 33 and 36.

and the numbers in the table show the percentage of that total trade that each country accounts for. Several interesting facts emerge from the data in this table.

Before the Montevideo Treaty came into effect, Argentina and Brazil together accounted for 64.9 per cent of total trade among the countries listed. However, in 1962, when the effect of the treaty began to be felt, the combined participation of the two countries dropped to 58 per cent and after some fluctuations in 1967 they still account for 56.6 per cent of the total. Argentina has held its position somewhat better than Brazil, although neither one has significantly slipped. Following them in importance was Chile which has maintained its position after some small fluctuations. Peru, after jumping to 12.1 per cent in 1962, has gone back to the position that it had before 1962 with 8.9 per cent of the total. There are no very significant changes in the relative positions of Paraguay, Uruguay, and Ecuador.

Only two of the nine countries seem to have changed their participation in the total intraregional trade significantly. Mexico increased its relative importance from 1.2 per cent before 1962 to 6.0 per cent in 1966 and 1967; in other words its relative importance increased fivefold. Colombia also increased its relative importance, although less than Mexico; it went from 1.9 per cent before 1962 to 4.3 per cent in 1967 after reaching a high of 8.5 per cent in 1966. The similarity, however, ends there. Although they both increased their participation, they did it with a very different import-export mix which is reflected in the different signs shown in their trade balances. In order to turn to this aspect of the problem, a breakdown of total trade into its two components, imports and exports, is needed. Table 36 shows this breakdown for the nine countries as well as the difference between the two amounts, which is known as the trade balance.

Degree of Industrialization and the Balance of Trade

If the degree of industrialization is taken as a criterion the countries in Table 36 can be classified into three clear-cut groups. One group could be considered relatively more advanced; it includes Argentina, Brazil, and Mexico. The second group, in which industrialization is still at a very incipient state, and which could be called (borrowing an expression used by LAFTA economists) "relatively less developed," includes Ecuador and Paraguay. The third group comprises those countries which are at a much more advanced industrial stage than the second group, but because of different circumstances have not achieved the diversified industrial structure or the mass production of the countries in the first group. The secretariat of LAFTA believes that the main reason these countries have not moved to the first group is because of the size of the market, and consequently it has called them "countries of insufficient market." For the sake of simplicity they will be called here the intermediate group: Colombia, Chile, Peru, and Uruguay.

The figures in Table 36 seem to indicate that there is a close relationship between the degree of industrialization and the trade balance of the countries. The industrialized countries, Argentina and Mexico in particular, enjoy large and favorable balances; the small nonindustrial countries have small but positive balances; the intermediate countries have seen their balance deteriorate and at present all have large trade deficits vis-à-vis the rest of the region. There are explanations for this disparity, and it seems worthwhile to point them out.

The large countries of the area have developed an industrial sector that is somewhat more diversified and sophisticated than that of the other countries. Consequently, a greater number and variety of manufactures are produced, thus making their depend-

TABLE 36

Evolution of Intra-LAFTA Trade[a] by Country (In Million $)

Country	1957-61 Average	1962	1963	1964	1965	1966	1967
Colombia							
Exports	5.9	8.2	6.9	13.1	19.9	32.2	23.1
Imports	10.8	14.1	22.4	34.9	39.2	58.1	37.9
Balance	−4.9	−5.9	−15.5	−21.8	−19.3	−25.9	−14.8
Argentina							
Exports	130.6	141.4	185.0	218.4	231.1	242.7	271.4
Imports	138.3	103.2	101.6	170.7	255.7	226.7	212.0
Balance	−7.7	38.2	83.4	47.8	−24.5	16.0	59.4
Brazil							
Exports	107.9	75.8	76.0	132.8	197.4	181.5	154.2
Imports	98.2	128.6	163.9	168.0	190.4	167.0	171.6
Balance	9.7	−52.8	−87.9	−35.2	7.0	14.5	−17.4
Chile							
Exports	34.3	39.4	49.3	54.5	53.2	53.7	84.0[b]
Imports	66.9	80.5	120.0	128.9	122.1	140.9	140.0[b]
Balance	32.6	−41.1	−70.7	−74.4	−68.9	−87.2	−56.0[b]
Ecuador							
Exports	7.0	6.1	8.0	11.1	13.2	12.5	14.8
Imports	2.9	3.9	5.2	7.6	10.0	8.3	12.5
Balance	4.1	2.2	2.8	3.5	3.2	4.2	2.3
Mexico							
Exports	5.6	16.7	25.9	34.0	36.3	56.7	47.7
Imports	3.5	6.1	10.8	17.3	29.7	33.7	38.2
Balance	2.1	10.6	15.1	16.7	6.6	23.0	9.5
Paraguay							
Exports	10.5	10.9	10.7	14.5	17.6	20.0	15.6
Imports	9.1	6.1	8.4	11.6	13.3	14.3	16.5
Balance	1.4	4.8	2.3	2.9	4.3	5.7	0.9
Peru							
Exports	38.6	48.8	49.1	65.5	54.1	52.3	34.2
Imports	26.2	45.2	62.0	58.9	80.9	91.5	93.4
Balance	12.4	3.6	−12.9	6.6	−26.8	−39.2	−59.2
Uruguay							
Exports	7.1	8.0	15.0	15.0	15.6	26.8	17.0
Imports	32.4	34.0	31.8	48.4	32.1	46.0	44.1
Balance	−25.3	−26.0	−16.8	−33.4	−16.5	−19.2	−27.1

Source: LAFTA, *ALALC Síntesis Mensual* (Feb., 1968).
a. Venezuela and Bolivia are not included in LAFTA statistics due to their late start in the negotiations.
b. Estimates based on data for the first nine months.

ence on imports rather small as far as intermediate inputs are concerned. Their dependence on outside suppliers is then concentrated on capital goods which in most cases are not produced in the area (or if they are, the large countries produce them) and on some primary commodities which are frequently in surplus in the world market and whose prices are usually on the decline. They can also find a greater variety of intermediate products to export to the area.

The very small and relatively less developed countries (Ecuador and Paraguay) import a great amount of consumer goods. Since production of these goods does not require a very complex industrial sector, they are for the most part produced within the area and the small countries import a great proportion of them from their LAFTA partners. On the other hand, the small countries, not being industrialized, do not import large quantities of intermediate products. They can therefore adjust imports according to the receipts from the exports from their primary commodities since by doing so employment will not be reduced significantly but the standard of living of some people in the upper income brackets will be.

The countries in the intermediate group are in the middle of a squeeze. Their exports consist almost entirely of primary commodities whose problems were mentioned above. Their exports of manufactures or semimanufactures are subject to competition from the larger countries within the area, and the creation of new markets is made more difficult by the continued struggle for import substitution within each country. On the other hand, they must import a large amount of intermediate inputs to keep their production machinery going and avoid unemployment which would bring serious political and social consequences. Since they import hardly any consumer goods, the easiest way to reduce the trade gap is to reduce imports of capital goods. However, this does not affect intraregional trade because most of the capital equipment comes from outside the area. Therefore they tend to maintain a trade deficit with the rest of LAFTA. Colombia's deficit has increased from nearly $5 million before the treaty to $25.9 million in 1966 and $14.8 in 1967. Chile and Peru saw a surplus in the period 1957–61 turn into heavy deficits after trade liberalization took place. Uruguay has maintained its deficit at about the same level, even though it has been going through one of its worst economic crises over the last three years and the government has tried many kinds of import restrictions.

It seems, then, that the expansion in intraregional trade, which is so loudly proclaimed by the advocates of LAFTA, has taken place at the expense of the intermediate size countries of which Colombia is one. The persistence of this imbalance in the trade patterns of LAFTA could turn into one of the greatest obstacles to economic integration: the formation within the region of one block of countries with a persistent trade surplus and another with a persistent trade deficit. Thus we would have a scale model of the situation existing in the world and which led, in part, to the creation of LAFTA.

Colombia's Balance with LAFTA

The figures in Table 36 indicate that Colombia's exports to LAFTA countries have not increased as fast as its imports from them. A comparison of the five years before the Montevideo Treaty with the most recent years of trade shows that imports have increased from $10.9 million for the annual average during 1957–61 to a high of $58.1 million in 1966 and $37.9 million in 1967. Exports on the other hand have only reached a maximum of $32.2 million in 1966 and in 1967 they were valued at $23.1 million. This disparity in the growth of imports and exports has caused the trade deficit to increase continuously.

A trade deficit with the region per se should not be a matter of much concern unless it brings with it some economic disadvantages (larger disbursements of foreign exchange, undesirable changes in the import structure, et cetera). If there has been only a change in the sources of supply, the region as a whole will benefit without detriment to the country's economy. True, less will be collected by the government for custom duties, but this will be compensated for by lower prices to the consumer. What should be of concern is whether the countries that have enjoyed an increased share of the Colombian market have in turn tried to stimulate imports from Colombia or whether "reciprocal benefits" implicit in the Montevideo Treaty have been a one-way street. If the latter has been the case Colombia would be justified in adjusting its imports pattern in a manner that would benefit those countries whose imports from it have increased or have shown a structure that stimulates the manufacturing sector. After all, the very purpose of Latin American integration is to stimulate industrial activity and take advantage of a larger market. The nature of Colombia's trade deficit with the region can be disclosed better by analyzing the trade on a country by country basis.[1] This will be the next task.

Colombia's Trade with Argentina

Table 37 summarizes the trade between Colombia and Argentina on a yearly basis. Before trade liberalization occurred Colombia enjoyed a positive balance of trade with that country, although it was rather insignificant. Trade was limited to some exports of coffee and pit-coal tar and imports of oats, wheat, and raw wool. After 1962, trade expanded very rapidly in both directions. Imports of raw wool increased considerably, reaching almost $3.5 million

TABLE 37

TRADE BALANCE WITH ARGENTINA (IN THOUSAND $)

Year	Exports	Imports	Balance
1957–61 average	412	323	89
1962	692	2,375	−1,683
1963	623	8,628	−8,005
1964	3,400	8,800	−5,400
1965	5,454	9,840	−4,386
1966	11,718	13,161	−1,443
1967	4,507	8,785	−4,278

SOURCE: LAFTA, *ALALC Síntesis Mensual,* several issues.

in 1966, but were surpassed in that year by lard, which became Argentina's main export, worth $6.8 million. Other products became somewhat important, mainly oats, the value of which fluctuated between $100,000 and $300,000 per year, linseed oil ($300,000–$400,000), and quebracho ($300,000–$500,000).

Exports to Argentina not only increased substantially during the period, but what is more important, they diversified significantly. Colombian coffee made a sizeable dent in what used to be almost an exclusive Brazilian market, and by 1966 the exports of this commodity were valued at over $5.5 million. Next in importance were automobile tires which fluctuated between $1 and $3.6 million per year making Argentina the largest single importer of this important Colombian manufactured good. Another manufacture which became an important export was plastic cables, reaching over $1 mil-

1. The information regarding the main products that are imported from and exported to the different countries has been extracted from several issues of *Boletín Mensual de Estadística* published by DANE.

lion in 1966. Pit-coal tar held its importance, fluctuating between $50,000 and $361,000. Other new products exported in 1966 were dry batteries ($430,000), typewriters ($115,000), and fungicides ($260,800).

Since 1962, the trade balance has been favorable to Argentina, but trade with this country has been a dynamic factor from the Colombian point of view. Imports consist mainly of raw commodities which were imported from other sources prior to 1962, while exports, with the exception of coffee, have been made up mainly of industrial items. On the basis of reciprocity Argentina should continue to be a good market for Colombian manufactures since imports of lard and raw wool should continue at least for the next few years. However, coffee is a different matter; since Brazil is the main

TABLE 38

Trade Balance with Brazil (In Thousand $)

Year	Exports	Imports	Balance
1957–61 average	118	304	−186
1962	15	148	−133
1963	129	543	−414
1964		1,900	−1,900
1965	377	3,108	−2,731
1966	460	7,344	−6,884
1967	561	2,932	−2,371

Source: lafta, ALALC Síntesis Mensual, several issues.

market for Argentina's wheat there may be political pressures to limit imports from Colombia. In 1967 exports of coffee to Argentina dropped nearly $3 million with respect to 1966. It is hard to predict what the future trade will be, but in all fairness it must be said that Colombia–Argentina trade has been beneficial to both.

Colombia's Trade with Brazil

During the five-year period from 1957 to 1961 Colombia's exports to Brazil averaged $118,000 per year while imports averaged $304,000 per year, leaving a balance of $186,000 in favor of Brazil (Table 38). This situation did not change significantly in 1962 or 1963. Starting in 1964, however, there has been a large increase in imports from Brazil which has not been matched by a similar increase in exports to that country. From 1964 to 1967 Colombia has accumulated a deficit of more than $13 million, half of which occurred in 1966 alone.

Colombian exports to Brazil, which barely surpassed the $500,000 figure in 1967 (the best year so far), are made up mainly of cement and naphthenic acid. Some beef has been exported sporadically in very small amounts, and in 1967 a new item, speakers for radios and other uses, was exported with a value of $13,700.

The largest single import from Brazil is raw cacao, which in 1966 accounted for $5.3 million. Other important items, with the amount corresponding to 1966 in parentheses, have been pepper ($178,000), flat copper wire ($132,000), razors ($86,000), and copper-lined steel pipes ($87,000). Some metal-working machinery has been imported but not consistently.

The future of Colombian trade with Brazil is very uncertain. So far Brazil has not made any steps toward closing the trade gap,

TABLE 39

TRADE BALANCE WITH MEXICO (IN THOUSAND $)

Year	Exports	Imports	Balance
1957–61 average	95	891	−796
1962	108	1,649	−1,541
1963	216	3,112	−2,896
1964	300	4,500	−4,200
1965	517	5,807	−5,290
1966	649	9,895	−9,246
1967	367	5,549	−5,182

SOURCE: LAFTA, *ALALC Síntesis Mensual*, several issues.

and the Colombian delegation to LAFTA has been unsuccessful in obtaining concessions for several products which might be exported competitively to that market, among them, asphalt tile, aluminum manufactures, and equipment for fumigating and fire extinguishing. Trade liberalization in this case seems to have worked in favor of Brazil only, and Colombia should explore the implications of substituting cacao from Ecuador for that from Brazil provided that Ecuador's production is elastic enough.

Colombia's Trade with Mexico

This is another case in which trade liberalization seems to have worked one way only. The balance of trade with Mexico has always been negative and shows a tendency to become more so. Table 39 shows that imports increased from an average of $796,000 per year prior to 1962 to almost $5.2 million in 1967, after reaching a peak of $9.2 million in 1966. During the same period exports only increased to a maximum of $649,000 in 1966 and in 1967 they were $367,000. The negative balance accumulated during the last four years of trade is even higher than that with Brazil, being slightly under $20 million.

If the dollar figures of the trade with Mexico are discouraging, the composition of that trade does not seem any better. Exports are composed almost entirely of two raw materials, fuel oil and lumber, and one chemical, naphthenic acid, which in 1966 accounted for only $57,000. That same year fuel oil accounted for $431,500 and lumber for $101,400. These three products, then, made up 90 per cent of total exports.

Colombian imports from Mexico were considerably more diversified than its exports, although most of them belonged to the groups of chemicals, resins, and minerals with a substantial amount of elaborated metallic products; raisins and raw cotton accounted for the remainder. Table 40 is a list of the main products imported from Mexico and their value in 1966.

It is obvious that trade with Mexico has not stimulated the industrial sectors of the Colombian economy. Due to the more advanced technology existing in Mexico, under present conditions Colombian imports will keep growing faster than its exports and, wherever possible, Colombia might do well to substitute imports from Mexico for imports from other countries where trade is taking place on more reciprocal grounds. Preliminary data seem to indicate that to some extent this process is taking place (see "Colombia's Trade with Venezuela" below).

Colombia's Trade with Uruguay

Colombia's trade with Uruguay has always favored the latter. The liberalization of trade has had the effect of increasing the imports from Uruguay considerably (from an average $367,000 prior to 1962 to as much as $6.8 million in 1966), while exports to that country have remained at very low levels (Table 41). Trade is concentrated in very few products with raw wool accounting for over 90 per cent of all Colombian imports ($6.4 million in 1966), and lard and tallow accounting for the rest. Colombian exports have been limited to coffee, artificial yarn, and tobacco.

The present economic situation of Uruguay, its lack of available foreign exchange, and its close economic and historical ties to a competitive supplier of manufactures, Argentina, seems to indicate that no market of importance for Colombian products will develop there in the near future. Colombia, on the other hand, will probably continue to import raw wool in the next few years as the import substitution of this product is a long-run undertaking.

Colombia's Trade with Paraguay

Trade with Paraguay has been almost negligible (Table 42). Exports have consisted of stamps, paper money, and some chemi-

TABLE 40
MAIN IMPORTS FROM MEXICO, 1966

Item	C.I.F. Value ($)
Steel pipe for oil pipelines	1,535,000
Raw zinc	1,274,000
Chemicals and resins	1,024,000
Refined copper and copper alloys	438,000
Aluminum (raw and ingots)	354,000
Raw lead	318,000
Glass products	304,000
Raisins	256,000
Raw cotton	158,000

TABLE 41
TRADE BALANCE WITH URUGUAY (IN THOUSAND $)

Year	Exports	Imports	Balance
1957–61 average	20	367	− 347
1962	143	2,396	− 2,253
1963	285	1,717	− 1,432
1964	500	6,300	− 5,800
1965	279	5,860	− 5,581
1966	263	6,874	− 6,611
1967	91	2,735	− 2,644

SOURCE: LAFTA, *ALALC Síntesis Mensual*, several issues.

TABLE 42
TRADE BALANCE WITH PARAGUAY (IN THOUSAND $)

Year	Exports	Imports	Balance
1957–61 average			
1962	15		15
1963	38	3	35
1964			
1965	192	37	155
1966	188	19	169
1967	109	23	86

SOURCE: LAFTA, *ALALC Síntesis Mensual*, several issues.

cals while imports have been limited to printed books and some minor handcraft articles. Paraguay will not evolve as a market of importance for Colombia in the near future due to its low level of economic development and the difficulties of transport to that land-locked country.

Colombia's Trade with Chile

Total trade between Colombia and Chile could be classified as small in dollar terms when compared with trade with most of the other countries in LAFTA (Table 43), but it shows a tendency to grow and, what is more important, to diversify and include more manufactured goods. Prior to 1964 Colombian exports to Chile were overwhelmingly composed of two agricultural commodities,

TABLE 43

TRADE BALANCE WITH CHILE (IN THOUSAND $)

Year	Exports	Imports	Balance
1957–61 average	895	866	29
1962	990	204	786
1963	322	958	636
1964	300	1,500	−1,200
1965	755	2,296	−1,541
1966	1,262	3,488	−2,226
1967	1,854	1,719	135

SOURCE: LAFTA, *ALALC Síntesis Mensual*, several issues.

raw sugar and coffee. Exports of sugar were valued at $232,000 in 1961 and $419,000 in 1962, but after that year sugar from Argentina and Peru replaced Colombian sugar in the Chilean market. During 1963 and 1964 coffee was the main export followed by cotton and some pharmaceutical products. Starting in 1965 several manufactured products were added to the list; among them were plastic cables, typewriters, concrete mixers, dry batteries, electric cables, and some light earth-moving machinery. Beef was also added in 1966. Table 44 is a list of items accounting for over 95 per cent of the present total value of Colombian exports to Chile and their value in 1966.

Compared with the 1957–61 average then, Colombia has doubled the value of its exports to Chile and has changed their structure significantly, to the extent that raw agricultural commodities or livestock products, which accounted for over 90 per cent of total value prior to 1965, account for less than one-third at the present time.

Colombian imports from Chile consist mainly of some raw minerals, silicone and manganese, refined copper, wood paste, wines, oats, newspaper, paper for computer cards, and chemicals. The last three items are new additions to the import list and, at least in the case of the last two, their trade is a consequence of complementarity and special agreements resulting directly from the Montevideo negotiations.

Trade liberalization has been a dynamic factor in Colombia–Chile trade, and even though the overall balance seems to be slightly in favor of Chile, Colombia and its industrial sector have benefited from it.

TABLE 44

Main Exports to Chile, 1966

Item	F.O.B. Value ($)
Plastic cables	364,400
Coffee	211,900
Typewriters	183,800
Beef (frozen, chilled, and fresh)	180,000
Dry batteries	138,200
Earth-moving machinery	69,200
Concrete mixers	47,500
Electric cables	30,100

Colombia's Trade with Ecuador

Because of its geographic location Ecuador has always been an important trade partner of Colombia; as a matter of fact, prior to 1965 it was the largest buyer of Colombian products in Latin America. Before 1962 exports to Ecuador were composed primarily of raw cotton, cotton yarn, textiles, and pharmaceutical products, but since then this structure has changed significantly. Exports of raw cotton have disappeared and exports of cotton textiles have diminished considerably while synthetic yarns and fabrics have increased in importance. Many types of small machinery and equipment have been added to the list of exports and significant gains have been made in important areas like cement-asbestos products, paper products, glass manufactures, and iron and steel products. At the present time almost all of Colombia's exports to Ecuador are manufactured products. Table 45 lists the most important groups of items making up over 80 per cent of those exports and their value in 1966.

The imports from Ecuador do not show the same variety that exports to that country do. The imports have traditionally been overwhelmingly dominated by a single commodity, raw cacao. Since the Montevideo Treaty, however, there has been an increase

TABLE 45

MAIN EXPORTS TO ECUADOR, 1966

Item	F.O.B. Value ($)
Cement-asbestos products	1,027,200
Paper products	846,900
Medicines	797,200
Synthetic yarn	501,600
Glass products	353,100
Copper wire	254,000
Iron and steel manufactures	251,800
Cotton textiles	122,100
Ceramic manufactures	114,200
Aluminum manufactures	93,000
Plastic cables	88,800

TABLE 46

TRADE BALANCE WITH ECUADOR (IN THOUSAND $)

Year	Exports	Imports	Balance
1957–61 average	497	4,802	−4,305
1962	1,502	4,866	−3,364
1963	2,660	4,446	−1,786
1964	3,700	6,300	−2,600
1965	3,928	6,667	−2,739
1966	5,112	4,972	140
1967	5,613	5,902	−289

SOURCE: LAFTA, ALALC Síntesis Mensual, several issues.

in imports of medicines (antibiotics, vaccines) both for human and veterinary uses, which in 1966 were valued at $1.3 million. At present these two items account for over 95 per cent of total exports to Colombia.

Although the trade balance has consistently favored Ecuador (Table 46) there is no question that Colombia has greatly benefited from the negotiations regarding trade liberalization with that nation. Ecuador has become an important market for Colombian manufactures and as such it can be regarded as a dynamic element from the point of view of Colombia's trade. Since Colombia has traditionally been a good market for Ecuador's cacao and could become a better one by substituting more of it for Brazilian cacao, it is very likely that it could increase and diversify still more its sales to Ecuador without detriment to that country's trade balance with Colombia. Consequently, sales to Ecuador should continue strong over the near future.

Colombia's Trade with Peru

Like Ecuador, Peru has traditionally been an important trade partner of Colombia, and the figures in Table 47 indicate that trade in both directions shows an upward trend; the balance has shown no signs of consistently favoring either country. In value terms, then, it can be said that trade between Peru and Colombia is bal-

TABLE 47

TRADE BALANCE WITH PERU (IN THOUSAND $)

Year	Exports	Imports	Balance
1957–61 average	2,244	1,253	991
1962	3,841	884	2,957
1963	1,777	1,985	−208
1964	2,700	3,800	−1,100
1965	5,198	4,737	461
1966	9,461	10,276	−815
1967	5,660	4,279	1,381

SOURCE: LAFTA, ALALC Síntesis Mensual, several issues.

anced and growing. The structure of Colombian exports, however, seems to be much more diversified and modern than that of Peru.

Up to 1963 Colombian exports to Peru were composed mainly of two products, fuel oil and cotton textiles; some beef was exported but usually in minor quantities, and the rest of the export items never accounted for more than 10 per cent of the total. Starting in 1962, new products of industrial origin began to appear, while traditional exports of textiles experienced a substantial decrease. Fuel oil, although fluctuating considerably from year to year, still continues to be one of the most important single items. The first new industrial products to appear were cement ($146,200 in 1962), artificial yarn ($110,400 and $180,000 in 1962 and 1963, respectively), and pharmaceuticals ($57,300 in 1963). Since then a large number of manufactures have been added, and in 1966 the value of exports of products classified as processed or semiprocessed amounted to well over $2 million. Table 48 lists items accounting for over 90 per cent of Colombia's exports to Peru and their value in 1966.

Imports from Peru are almost totally made up of three types of products: fish and its derivatives, long staple cotton, and raw minerals. In 1966, 80 per cent of total imports belonged to the first category, 8 per cent to the second, and 2 per cent to the third. The remaining 10 per cent consisted of minor products of which alpaca tops and some steel pieces used in the manufacture of grain mills were the most important.

The same things that were said about Ecuador can be said about Peru and its trade with Colombia. Peru seems to have become a good market for Colombia's manufactures while Colombia buys a

TABLE 48

MAIN EXPORTS TO PERU, 1966

Item	F.O.B. Value ($)
Cattle (live for slaughter)	5,210,000
Fuel oil	2,301,700
Beef (fresh, frozen, chilled)	371,000
Cement	231,800
Paper products	192,351
Ceramic manufactures	164,800
Grain mills	162,600
Medicines	156,000
Vegetable cakes	134,900
Cotton textiles	121,700
Small machinery (pumps, concrete mixers, etc.)	100,000
Rubber products	45,000
Fiberglass products	22,000

substantial amount of products derived from the fishing industry which is vital to the economy of Peru and also long staple cotton of which there is usually a sizeable surplus in that country. Within a framework of reciprocity, Colombia can expect to increase its exports of manufactures to Peru and at the same time increase its imports. Although an increase in the import of fish products is not unlikely, most of the potential lies in long staple cotton, total imports of which amounted to $4.3 million in 1966, only $789,000 of which came from Peru.

Colombia's Trade with Venezuela

The study of Colombia–Venezuela trade is complicated by the fact that a very substantial amount of contraband activity takes place in both directions. Although this is also true in the cases of trade with Ecuador and Peru, illegal trade with these two countries seems to be minor compared with total registered trade. In the case of Venezuela, however, it has been estimated that contraband may reach as much as $50 million per year,[2] or many times the value of registered trade (Table 49). Illegal trade consists mainly of cattle going from Colombia to Venezuela due to a substantial difference in prices between the two countries and of coffee smuggled to Venezuela to be re-exported. From Venezuela to Colombia the illegal traffic is mainly in processed foodstuffs and household appliances which usually originate in third countries. Reduction of tariffs or restrictions would only incorporate to legal trade that part which corresponds to cattle. With this in mind let us take a look at the registered trade between the two countries.

TABLE 49

TRADE BALANCE WITH VENEZUELA (IN THOUSAND $)

Year	Exports	Imports	Balance
1957–61 average	1,623	2,049	−426
1962	927	1,621	−694
1963	883	1,012	−129
1964	2,192	1,758	434
1965	3,235	906	2,329
1966	3,046	2,022	1,024
1967	4,147	5,961	−1,814

SOURCE: DANE, *Anuario de Comercio Exterior*, several issues, and DANE, *Boletín Mensual de Estadística* (Mar., 1968).

Prior to 1964, exports to Venezuela consisted mainly of agricultural products, and the only manufactures that were exported to any extent were artificial yarn, some textiles, grain mills, and a few pharmaceutical products which were valued at $64,000 in 1962. Starting in 1964 a considerable amount of manufactured items have been added to the list, the most significant of which are tubes and other cement-asbestos manufactures, centrifugal pumps, iron and steel products, automobile springs, and plastic products. Other additions which do not belong to the group of manufactures are sugar and fighting bulls. Since Venezuela did not join LAFTA until 1966, the diversification of trade that took place in 1964 cannot be attributed to the Montevideo Treaty although indirectly it is a result of Colombian industry having become more aggressive and diversi-

2. Banco Interamericano de Desarrollo. *Posibilidades de Integración de las Zonas Fronterizas Colombo-Venezolanas*, p. 116.

fied and taking advantage of the favorable trade relations that have always existed between the two countries. A list of the most important items exported in 1966 and their value is given in Table 50.

The figures for the first months of 1967 seem to indicate that the value of trade for most of the above items increased. Cement-asbestos manufactures probably reached $2 million and paper products became important, totalling $125,000 for the first eleven months.

Imports from Venezuela were composed mainly of processed foodstuffs, lubricating oils, and certain minerals. Starting in 1966 the imports of seamless steel pipes for oil pipelines became important, reaching $405,000. During the first eleven months of 1967, the value of imports of this type of pipe had reached $5,228,330. The fact that this type of pipe had been previously imported from

TABLE 50

MAIN EXPORTS TO VENEZUELA, 1966

Item	F.O.B. Value ($)
Cement-asbestos manufactures	722,700
Grain mills	297,200
Sugarcane	267,500
Iron and steel joints, bolts, nuts, etc.	242,200
Water pumps	155,900
Steel pipes	113,900
Automobile springs	111,100
Raw zinc	61,800
Plastic products	60,000
Bulls for bullfighting	43,000

Mexico seems to indicate that Colombia may be starting to adopt a policy of substituting imports from its neighbors and good customers for imports from countries where its balance of trade shows a chronic deficit.

The trade balance with Venezuela in general has been favorable to Colombia although in 1967 it was not. This, however, is not important. What is important is that Colombia's manufactures seem to have broken into the Venezuelan market and that there are good trade prospects in both directions.

A Word of Caution

The discussion in this chapter has been carried on a two-way trade basis. The exports and imports of Colombia to and from each of the LAFTA countries before and after the Montevideo Treaty have been analyzed and the behavior of the balance of trade with each country and with the region as a whole has been studied. This approach is adequate for the purposes of this study but fails to show some of the causes behind the direction of Colombian trade. The analysis of this chapter shows for example that Colombia's purchases of Brazilian cacao have increased, but it does not give any hint as to why Colombia has chosen to buy part of its cacao from Brazil and not all from Ecuador, even though Brazil's imports from Colombia are very low while Ecuador is one of Colombia's best customers. It might happen that if Colombia reduced its imports of Brazilian cacao considerably, Brazil would try to force Argentina to reduce coffee imports from Colombia by threatening to cut its Argentina wheat imports.

In order to explore three-way relationships such as the one mentioned above, a complete analysis of intra-LAFTA trade would be necessary and this would be beyond the scope of this study. Therefore, a word of caution is necessary: the results of this chapter are adequate for analyzing the role of integration on the value of Colombia's trade with the region, but extreme care should be exercised in drawing trade policy implications from them.

7. Summary and Conclusions

IN THE LIST of priorities of a country, regardless of its state of development, there is one consideration for which the highest position is reserved and that is the economic and social betterment of its people. In the case of the less developed countries this preoccupation is augmented by the fact that their present standards are comparatively low and that they do not seem to be reaching their goals of improvement and progress. In fact, the gap between developed and underdeveloped countries is getting wider.

The economic development of Colombia over the last two decades has been slow, its rate of growth has been unstable, and the average per capita income expressed in real terms has increased less than 40 per cent as seen in chapter 3. If this pace continues, the 50 million Colombians will have, by the end of the century, an average annual income equivalent to $500 per capita, or approximately one-seventh of the income that an average resident of the United States enjoys presently. By that time, the United States should have a per capita income of over $8,500, assuming a conservative 3 per cent annual cumulative growth rate. In other words, today's ten to one ratio will become seventeen to one or more by the year 2000. It is very obvious, then, that Colombia is not participating adequately in the economic expansion that is taking place in most of the Free World and that, so far, it has not been able to bring about the economic and social conditions necessary for a rapid and self-sustained process of economic growth.

Some of the Factors Behind the Slow Growth

Several factors of different natures have contributed to the lack of dynamism shown by the Colombian economy. Among those factors that could be classified as of internal origin we may distinguish two kinds: social and economic. In considering the social factors, the most important of which were described in chapter 1, one encounters difficulty in determining which ones cause and which ones result in the failure to achieve a more desirable growth rate. Nevertheless, it can be stated that a low literacy rate, deficient health conditions, an undernourished population, and rural-urban migration that cannot be efficiently absorbed by slowly growing industry, together with a high rate of population growth, are all factors which hamper economic development and interfere with efforts to make the best use of the available physical and financial resources.

Some of the economic factors which interfere with rapid growth are: the uneven income distribution, which hinders efforts to increase the internal level of savings; the comparatively high rate of inflation, which erodes savings and slows economic activity; and the structure of the productive sectors of the economy, particularly the agricultural sector. Chapter 2 described the unequal distribution of land, the high percentage of farm population engaged in subsistence agriculture, the low level of technology reflected in low use of modern inputs, and the consequent low yields. The high degree of dependency on one crop, although determined by internal factors, affects development through prices which are determined externally.

The importance of all the above factors should not be underestimated. The government is aware that unless effective steps are taken to correct them, the goals for economic betterment will seem farther away. Some measures have already been taken: agrarian reform, health and sanitation drives, educational programs, and so forth. Nevertheless, the external sector of the economy is still a real bottleneck. Even if improvements are made in the internal socioeconomic conditions and even if the internal level of savings can be raised, foreign exchange must be available to pay for the investments that are necessary in order to keep building the infrastructure of the country. And because of the country's present stage of industrial development those needs will increase every year in the near future. Most of this study has been dedicated to the analysis of those factors which affect the availability and use of foreign exchange. It has explained how the region as a whole decided to integrate in order to attack a problem which is basically similar to the Colombian problem. In the introduction it was mentioned that, since the early stages of LAFTA, Colombia has been one of the most enthusiastic advocates of integration. Last, the changes that have taken place in the trade of Colombia with other LAFTA countries since the beginning of integration have been analyzed. It is time now to summarize the findings concerning the factors that affect the external sector and to take a look at the position of Colombia within the framework of LAFTA.

The Unfavorable External Sector

This study has shown how the industrialization process came about in Colombia, how the process of import substitution was stimulated, and how with the passage of time it became a deliberate government policy. One of the main results of this process was a considerable reduction in the imports of consumer goods. As was discussed in chapter 5, the proportion of total imports of consumer goods is of the order of 5 per cent of which less than 1.5 per cent is nondurables. The total level of import needs, however, did not diminish and an element of rigidity was added to the sector when industrialization occurred.

Because of protectionism and the characteristics of industry already discussed, and because the other Latin American countries were engaged in the same process, exports of manufactured goods were almost ruled out and most of the substitution was aimed at the internal market. Thus, although industrialization added a new facet to the economy and the participation of manufacturing industry in the gross domestic product increased, the country's dependence on agricultural commodities and minerals for obtaining needed foreign exchange remained basically unchanged.

It is well known that the prices of agricultural commodities in the world market, particularly those from tropical countries, have shown a declining tendency. This much publicized fact, plus the others just mentioned, caused a continuous deterioration in the balance of payments. From time to time the situation was corrected by external financing. However, this source of funds becomes more restrictive every year if the deficit in the balance is of a structural nature. A time comes when the existing obligations for servicing the foreign debt and the payments to foreign investment make it impossible to contract new ones.

External financing was no longer a feasible solution, import substitution in the feasible industries had been carried almost to the limit; the proceeds from the exports of traditional commodities could not be increased; the need for imports was not diminishing. This was the situation that Colombia was facing at the end of the fifties, the same situation that many other Latin American countries were facing. The attempt to solve these problems resulted in the resolutions of the Montevideo Treaty.

Colombia and LAFTA

The arguments in favor of economic integration in Latin America were given in the introduction and need not be repeated here; it is not intended to argue their general validity. However, on the basis of the data analyzed there are some questions about the timing and extent of economic integration as far as Colombia is concerned.

Colombia's primary consideration should be whether a continuation of the present patterns of trade within the region will bring it more economic benefits than a redistribution of this flow by subregional grouping or bilateral agreements. The second important consideration is whether the future industrialization and trade policies of the country should be tailored only on the basis of further integration among LAFTA countries or if a more ample policy which takes into consideration the economic ties with the United States and, to a lesser extent, the rest of the developed countries should be followed.

Regarding the second consideration it must be remembered that the analysis of the data shows that the dependence on the United States and the other developed nations for trade in the products in which Colombia seems to enjoy a certain comparative advantage is still overwhelming and that as a consequence there are many marketing channels that are already established, of which greater advantage could and must be taken. An increase of 10 per cent in the value of exports to the United States would have the same effect on the country's trade balance as doubling the exports to all

LAFTA countries. It will probably be easier to diversify exports through sales to developed countries with large purchasing power and where the competition will not cause the difficulties that might be created in countries with an economic structure similar to that of Colombia. In other words, "the problem of finding markets that will permit the expansion of the present industries, and the creation of new ones, should not be subordinated exclusively to the developments that take place within LAFTA as the experience of the last few years is painfully demonstrating."[1]

With regard to whether integration has brought any specific economic benefits to the country, the analysis of the data has shown that as far as the two largest markets in the region are concerned (Brazil and Mexico) the contribution to Colombia's trade balance has been neutral in the best of cases (that is if it is assumed that only a change in the source of supply took place); the same can be said with respect to Uruguay. Trade with Argentina has been more dynamic in the sense that a diversification in the products exported to that country can be observed even though a sizeable deficit has been accumulated through the period. Based on the principle of reciprocity, which is supposed to exist in an integration program, it has been argued that accumulating a deficit might stimulate the countries having a surplus to increase their imports from the deficit country in order to keep it as a customer. So far this has not been the case and, therefore, in this particular instance this proposition must be considered as being in the category of theory rather than fact.

Trade with the Andean countries, on the other hand, has been the most dynamic factor of integration. Exports to and imports from them have grown substantially, with exports growing slightly faster, thus resulting in a reduction of the trade deficit (Table 51). The Andean countries account for almost three-fourths of total Colombian exports to LAFTA and almost one-half of its total imports. The structure of that trade has evolved in favor of manufactured goods.

Two conclusions follow in light of the above evidence. First, more resources should be allocated to aggressive programs aimed at increasing the penetration and opening of new lines in the traditional markets, particularly the United States where some ground has been lost over the last decade. An effort to increase exports to

1. Carlos Lleras, *Comercio Internacional,* p. 278.

the rest of the world does not have to imply a neglect of the long-term possibilities that exist within the region.

Second, as far as trade with the region is concerned, the facts point out the potential benefits that Colombia could derive from an Andean subgroup. The evolution of trade among the Andean countries and its beneficial effects on the Colombian economy is itself a strong reason for Colombia to push this type of subregional integration, keeping in mind the observations at the end of chapter 6. Another favorable argument is that many of the obstacles that are stalling the overall integration of LAFTA would be lessened; the concern about different levels of economic development would

TABLE 51

TRADE BALANCE WITH THE ANDEAN COUNTRIES[a] (IN THOUSAND $)

Year	Exports	Imports	Balance
1957–61 average	5,259	8,970	−3,711
1962	7,260	7,575	−315
1963	5,642	8,401	−2,759
1964	8,892	13,358	−4,466
1965	13,116	14,606	−1,490
1966	18,881	20,758	−1,877
1967	17,274	17,861	−587

SOURCE: Calculated from Tables 43, 46, 47, and 49.
a. Venezuela, Ecuador, Peru, and Chile (trade with Bolivia is negligible).

have less influence as most countries in the group are at similar stages; transportation difficulties would be eased; the clearing of payments would take less resources since trade among the Andean countries is more balanced than among LAFTA as a whole; and the narrow national markets would be expanded to one market of 60 million people with a purchasing power of $25 billion. A successful integration of the Andean countries would, among other things, remove the fear that all the benefits of regional integration would be reaped by Argentina, Brazil, and Mexico. When the question of moving on from a free trade area to a common market becomes urgent—perhaps during the decade of the eighties—the Andean bloc will be able to face the more developed countries of the region on more equal terms.

Bibliography

Asociación Latino Americana de Libre Comercio. *ALALC Síntesis Mensual.* Montevideo, 1966–68.

————. *Tratado de Montevideo, Resoluciones de la Conferencia.* Montevideo, 1963.

Balassa, Bela. *The Theory of Economic Integration.* Homewood, Ill.: Richard D. Irwin, 1961.

Banco de la República. *Cuentas Nacionales.* Bogotá, 1950–67.

Banco Interamericano de Desarrollo. *Posibilidades de Integración de las Zonas Fronterizas Colombo-Venezolanas.* Washington: Interamerican Development Bank, 1964.

————. *El Desarrollo Económico y la Integración.* México: Centro de Estudios Monetarios Latino-Americano, 1965.

Caja de Crédito Agrario Industrial y Minero, Departamento de Investigaciones Economicas. *Mecanización Agrícola en Colombia.* Bogotá, 1965 (mimeograph).

Currie, Lauchlin. *Bases de un Programa de Fomento para Colombia.* Bogotá: Banco de la República, 1951.

De Aguiar, Pinto. *Fundamentos, Objectivos e Bases do Mercado Regional Latino-Americano.* Bahia: Universidade de Bahia, 1958.

Dell, Sidney S. *Problemas de un Mercado Común en América Latina.* Mexico: Centro de Estudios Monetarios Latino Americanos, 1959.

Departamento Administrativo Nacional de Estadística (DANE). *Anuario de Comercio Exterior.* Bogotá, 1950–66.

————. *Anuario General de Estadística.* Bogotá, 1950–67.

————. *Boletín Mensual de Estadística.* Bogotá, 1957–68.

————. *Censo Agropecuario Nacional.* Bogotá, 1960.

————. *Censo de Población de Colombia 1951, Resumen.* Bogotá, 1952.

————. *Censo Nacional de Población, Julio 15 de 1964, Resumen General.* Bogotá, 1964.

————. *Directorio Nacional de Explotaciones Agropecuarias, Resumen Nacional Segunde Parte.* Bogotá, 1964.

————. *Encuesta Agropecuaria Nacional 1965.* Bogotá, 1966.

————. *Informe al Congreso Nacional.* Bogotá, 1963.

Domar, D. Evsey. "Expansion and Employment." *American Economic Review* (Mar., 1947), pp. 34–55.

Food and Agriculture Organization of the United Nations. *Production Yearbook,* vol. 20. Rome, 1966.

Furtado, Celso. *Development and Underdevelopment.* Berkeley: University of California Press, 1964.

Harrod, Roy. "An Essay in Dynamic Theory." *Economic Journal* (Mar., 1939), pp. 14–33.

Hume, David. "On the Balance of Trade." Reprinted in *International Trade Theory,* ed. William Allen. N.Y.: Random House, 1965.

International Monetary Fund. *International Financial Statistics.* Washington, Dec. 1968.

Lleras, Carlos. *Comercio Internacional.* Medellín: Instituto Colombiano de Administración, 1965.

Marshall, Alfred. *The Pure Theory of Foreign Trade.* London: London School of Economics and Political Science, 1930.

Mill, John Stuart. *Principles of Political Economy.* London: Longmans, Green & Co., 1923.

Naciones Unidas, Comisión Económica para América Latina. *Bases para la Formación de un Mercado Común Latino-Americano.* Mexico, 1958.

————. *Estudio Económico de América Latina.* Santiago, 1957.

————. *El Mercado Común Latino Americano.* México, 1959.

Organization of American States. *Domestic Exports and the Needs for External Financing for the Development of Colombia.* Washington, 1968.

Plan Nacional de Pesca. Departamento Nacional de Planeacion Bogotá Planning Department Paper. Bogotá, 1967.

Ricardo, David. *The Principles of Political Economy and Taxation.* London: J. M. Dent and Sons, 1911.

Smith, Adam. *An Inquiry into the Nature and Causes of the Wealth of Nations.* N.Y.: Random House, 1937.

Solow, R. M. "Technical Change and the Aggregate Production Function." *Review of Economics and Statistics* (Aug., 1957), pp. 312–20.

United Nations, Economic Commission for Latin America. *Economic Survey of Latin America.* N.Y., 1965.

————. *The Economic Development of Latin America in the Post-War Period.* N.Y., 1964.

————. *The Process of Industrial Development of Latin America.* N.Y., 1966.

————. *Statistical Bulletin of Latin America,* vol. 3, nos. 1, 2. N.Y., 1966.

Urquidi, Victor L. *Trayectoria del Mercado Común Latino Americano.* Mexico: Centro de Estudios Monetarios Latino Americano, 1960.

————. *Viabilidad Económica de América Latina.* Mexico: Fondo de Cultura Económica, 1962.

Wionczeck Miguel S. *Integración de la América Latina.* Mexico: Fondo de Cultura Económica, 1964.

LATIN AMERICAN MONOGRAPHS—SECOND SERIES